SYRIA
BURNING

A Short History of a Catastrophe

CHARLES GLASS

With a foreword by Patrick Cockburn

VERSO
London • New York

This updated edition first published by Verso 2016
First published by OR Books 2015
© Charles Glass 2015, 2016
Foreword © Patrick Cockburn 2015, 2016

13 5 7 9 10 8 6 4 2

Verso
UK: 6 Meard Street, London W1F 0EG
US: 20 Jay Street, Suite 1010, Brooklyn, NY 11201
versobooks.com

Verso is the imprint of New Left Books

ISBN-13: 978-1-78478-516-1
ISBN-13: 978-1-78478-518-5 (US EBK)
ISBN-13: 978-1-78478-517-8 (UK EBK)

British Library Cataloguing in Publication Data
A catalogue record for this book is available from the British Library

Library of Congress Cataloging-in-Publication Data
A catalog record for this book is available from the Library of Congress

Printed in the US by Maple Press

For Lucien,
with love from Dad

and in memory of Armen Mazloumian,
proprietor of the Baron's Hotel in Aleppo,
who refused to abandon his city and
died there on January 15, 2016

CONTENTS

FOREWORD

THE WAR IN SYRIA HAS LONG NEEDED A good book to explain what and why it is happening. Few events in recent history have been subjected to so much inadequate and partial reporting and there are few writers who have the perception and experience to illuminate this terrible tragedy. Charles Glass is one of them: he knows Syria, Lebanon and the region extremely well and has been an eyewitness to its crises and wars since the 1970s. He has essential recent experience gained through his travels to Damascus, Aleppo, Homs and other parts of Syria since the conflict started in 2011 and a popular revolt rapidly transformed into a sectarian civil war.

It is difficult to write sensibly and with balance about a struggle in which all sides, including much of the media, is so partisan. From the early days of the Arab Spring, not just in Syria but in other countries caught up in these complex developments, journalists often crudely demonized one side and portrayed the other as unblemished democrats. Obvious contradictions were ignored: how, for instance, could the Syrian rebels be the secular democrats they purported to be when their most important supporters and financiers were Saudi Arabia, Qatar and the oil-states of the Gulf, whose rulers are the last theocratic absolute monarchies left on earth?

The media was not alone in its self-deception. Leaders in the US, Europe and the region assumed that President Bashar al-Assad would fall in 2011 or early 2012 because they had just seen Muammar Gaddafi overthrown and killed. This was despite the fact that, at his weakest, Assad controlled thirteen out of fourteen of Syria's provincial capitals. Only full scale US intervention, more along the lines of Iraq in 2003 than Libya in 2011, would have overthrown him. Rebels pretended that all they needed was some heavy weaponry and a few US air strikes to win, but this was never the case.

The Syrian war is today frequently compared to the Thirty Years War in Germany in the seventeenth century and, unlike many such historic analogies, this one reveals an important truth. As in Germany four hundred years ago, there are now so many players with divergent interests in Syria that the conflict is becoming impossible to end. Syrians have less and less influence over the fate of their country. To understand all this is not easy, and anybody who tries to do so must combine deep understanding of the region with up-to-date knowledge at ground level from one of the most dangerous places on earth. In this study, Charles Glass tells us more about the reality of Syria and its future than could be gained from any other single source.

— *Patrick Cockburn*

CHRONOLOGY

2011: Harsh government suppression fans local demonstrations into a mass civil uprising and isolates the regime abroad.

March–June
Protesters in Dera'a demand the release of a dozen teenagers who have been arrested for anti-regime graffiti and tortured. Security forces open fire, killing several demonstrators. This escalates and radicalizes the demonstrations, which spread to Damascus, Homs, Idlib and other population centers. President Bashar al-Assad pursues a two-pronged strategy, promising political reform while overseeing harsh military crackdowns on the protests. In May, government tanks move against demonstrators in

Dera'a and the suburbs of Damascus, as well as in Homs, which has become the center of the uprising. The opposition's call for a national strike is largely ignored in Syria's two most populous cities, Damascus and Aleppo. The following month sees government troops besiege the town of Jisr al-Shughour. The regime's brutal suppression provokes increasing international condemnation and in May the US and EU impose sanctions.

July–October

In July, Syrian security forces reportedly kill more than 100 protesters in Hama. US Secretary of State Hillary Clinton declares that Assad has "lost legitimacy." The crackdown pressures the Syrian opposition to become organized and militarized. Military defectors establish the Free Syrian Army (FSA) in July and in October, six months into the uprising, some opposition groups coalesce as the Syrian National Council (SNC). Its declared aim is to topple Assad within six months. The UN Security Council condemns "widespread violations of human rights and the use of force against civilians by the Syrian authorities," but Russia and China veto a resolution threatening sanctions.

November–December

The Arab League suspends Syria and imposes sanctions. France calls for western military intervention, while Russia continues to arm the regime. Armed conflict between the FSA and regime soldiers is becoming the dominant dynamic on the ground, and in November the FSA launches a high-profile attack on a military base near Damascus. In December, two car bombs in Damascus kill 44 people—the opposition blames the regime, while the Syrian government and, later, US officials finger al-Qaeda. An Arab League observer mission enters Syria.

♦

2012: The conflict escalates to all-out civil war. Foreign assistance to both sides fuels the violence and adds proxy wars to the internal conflict.

January–April

The Arab League observer mission withdraws in January, citing increasing violence. The same month sees the birth of a new rebel military faction, the al-Qaeda-affiliated al-Nusra Front, and in a videotape released soon afterward al-Qaeda's Ayman al-Zawahiri urges Sunni Muslims to support the Syrian revolt. In February, the UN General Assembly votes 137-12 for Assad to resign. Russia and China veto a similar resolution at the Security Council. The "Group of Friends of the Syrian People," a collection of more than 60 (later rising to more than 100) countries and organizations including France, Britain, Saudi Arabia, Turkey and the United States, proclaims the SNC a "legitimate representative" of Syria. The EU announces new sanctions, while former UN Secretary-General Kofi Annan is appointed UN–Arab League Special Envoy to Syria. Government forces and the FSA contend for control in Homs, Damascus and other major cities. In April, the "Friends of Syria" pledge economic support for opposition forces, while Saudi Arabia and the Gulf states announce a new fund for the FSA. A ceasefire brokered by Annan does not stem the violence.

May–July

In May, the Security Council unanimously condemns the regime's use of heavy weapons in Houla, which killed dozens of civilians in Houla. In July, the International Committee of the Red Cross declares the situation in Syria a civil war. Fighting is intense in Idlib, Damascus, Deir Ezzor, Homs, Hama and Dera'a. Battling for control in Damascus, rebel forces bomb the capital's National Security HQ, killing and injuring several senior officials including the Defense Minister and Deputy Defense Minister. The US and UK announce new sanctions against regime officials, but China and Russia veto a Security Council Chapter VII resolution. Major fighting breaks out in Aleppo when opposition forces blow up the government security headquarters and occupy parts of the city. The Syrian Army and Air Force attack the rebel positions in Aleppo.

August–October
The Kurds now control much of a Kurdish-speaking belt in northeast Syria under an agreement with the Syrian government. An August UN General Assembly resolution denounces Assad's use of heavy weaponry in Aleppo and Damascus. The regime suffers a few high-level defections. The UN pulls out of

Aleppo due to increasing violence. An incompetent Kofi Annan resigns as international envoy, and is replaced by the veteran Algerian diplomat and former foreign minister, Lakhdar Brahimi. President Obama identifies the use of chemical or biological weapons as a "red line" that may trigger military action. In September, the FSA launches a major offensive in Aleppo; a month later, much of the city's historic market and the ancient Omayyad Mosque are destroyed by fire and shelling. In October, Secretary of State Clinton dismisses the SNC as lacking a base inside the country and "no longer...the visible leader of the opposition."

November–December
Syrian opposition groups, including the SNC, establish the National Coalition for Syrian Revolutionary and Opposition Forces. In December, the US declares the Nusra Front a terrorist organization and accuses it of trying to "hijack" the uprising. Turkey refuses to classify Nusra as a terrorist group. The US accuses Assad of using Scud missiles, and joins Turkey, France, the UK and the Gulf states in

formally recognizing the National Coalition as Syria's legitimate representative. Heavy fighting sees opposition forces take control of most of the Yarmouk Palestinian refugee camp in Damascus.

◆

2013: Jihadists increasingly dominate the opposition, as the regime regains the military initiative.

January–April
Assad rebuffs international demands to step down. Fighting continues in population centers across the country. After opposition forces capture the city of Raqqa in March, the US and UK promise non-military aid to the rebels. In April, the Syrian Army and Hezbollah launch a major offensive to retake the strategically crucial town of Qosair. Abu Bakr al-Baghdadi, self-proclaimed "emir" or prince of al-Qaeda in Iraq, claims responsibility for establishing the Nusra Front, and announces the groups' merger as the Islamic State in Iraq and the Levant (ISIS). The leader of the Nusra Front and al-Qaeda's al-Zawahiri reject the move.

May–August

The UN updates its estimate of the conflict death toll to 80,000, as the EU ends its embargo on arming the rebels. Government forces capture Qosair, a major strategic victory. The conflict continues to reverberate in Lebanon, where two rockets strike a Hezbollah stronghold in Beirut. Divisions within Syrian opposition forces widen, and in July ISIS assassinates two FSA commanders. In August, Islamist forces including the Nusra Front and ISIS attack Alawite villages in Latakia province, committing serious atrocities, but their territorial gains are short lived. President Obama announces that the US will bomb Syria, but only after Congressional approval. Opposition forces capture a military airport north of Aleppo and the towns of Ariha and Khanasir, severing regime supply lines to Aleppo. On August 30, the British parliament votes against military intervention in Syria.

September–December

The US Administration backs down from attacking Syria. UN inspectors report that chemical weapons have been used in Damascus. Opposition forces, including the Nusra Front, seize the Christian town of Maalula, but it is quickly retaken by the Syrian Army. The Security Council unanimously calls for the destruction of Syria's chemical weapons arsenal, and Assad permits international inspectors to begin the process in October. The regime launches two major offensives, which yield major gains around Damascus and Aleppo. Al-Zawahiri orders the dismantling of ISIS, which Baghdadi rejects. In December, the US and UK suspend "non-lethal assistance" to rebels in northern Syria after jihadists seize FSA bases.

◆

2014: Military and diplomatic stalemate drags as the death count rises. A major ISIS breakthrough in Iraq triggers a radical shift in international priorities.

January–May
The Islamic Front coalition of Salafist rebel groups and FSA forces launch an offensive against ISIS, and

after al-Zawahiri distances al-Qaeda from ISIS in February, the al-Nusra Front joins the fray. In March, jihadist groups and FSA elements from Turkey conquer the Syrian Armenian town of Kessab. Worldwide outrage and Armenian pressure compel Turkey to declare the Nusra Front a terrorist group. The Syrian Army drive the jihadists out a month later, and the inhabitants return. Two rounds of peace talks in Geneva convened by UN Secretary-General Ban Ki-moon achieve nothing. By a unanimous vote, the Security Council demands that all parties to the conflict cease attacks on civilians, singling out for censure the use of barrel bombs in populated areas. In May, a three-year battle for Homs ends in victory for the government, which permits rebel forces to evacuate the city. Special Envoy Brahimi resigns.

June–August

ISIS achieves a dramatic military breakthrough in Iraq, capturing the major cities of Mosul and Tikrit. It renames itself the Islamic State (IS) and proclaims a global caliphate. Assad holds a presidential election in government-controlled areas, winning nearly 90 percent of the vote, and international inspectors complete the removal of chemical weapons. Staffan de Mistura is appointed Brahimi's successor as UN special envoy for Syria. Human Rights Watch condemns the regime's continued use of barrel bombs in Aleppo. In August, the Nusra Front captures the Quneitra Crossing into the Israeli-occupied Golan Heights. IS reportedly massacres hundreds of people in Deir Ezzor province, while in Iraq, it captures the towns of Zumar, Wana and the Sinjar hills. IS kidnaps hundreds of Yazidi women, whom its militants rape or force into unwanted marriages. An IS siege of hundreds of Yazidi civilians on Mount Sinjar is broken by US air strikes and Kurdish fighters on August 14. The US begins arming Iraqi-Kurdish forces and, along with a coalition of international forces, commences air strikes on ISIS in Iraq. The US has now gone from calling for Assad's downfall to bombing his regime's opponents. On August 24, IS seizes the Syrian military airfield of Tabqa, completing the group's control of Raqqa province. IS proceeds to loot and destroy antiquities in Syria and Iraq, some dating to the second millennium B.C.

September–December

IS invests the Kurdish town of Kobani in Syria. Kurdish fighters, aided by international air strikes, repel IS forces from most of the town. The Israeli-American journalist Steven Sotloff is executed by IS. IS continues to attack from bases in Turkey. The Syrian Army presses on north of Aleppo until it controls all major supply lines to the city. It captures the strategically important town of Morek in October. In November, the Nusra Front captures Nawa from the Syrian Army and IS downs a Syrian Air Force fighter jet, while regime air strikes in Raqqa kill dozens. The American aid worker Peter Kassig is beheaded by IS. By December, it is widely accepted that the armed opposition will not succeed in toppling Assad.

◆

2015: The Islamic State and other jihadist forces make territorial gains and losses, while the regime loses the initiative it had seemed to hold the year before. Meanwhile, international intervention increases, with Russia, France and Arab countries launching airstrikes.

January–March

After four months of fighting, Kurdish forces retake the city of Kobane in northern Syria from IS in late January. They then advance into the Islamists' stronghold of Raqqa Province for the first time. Meanwhile, Syrian regime airstrikes kill 65 people in east Damascus, and loyalist forces execute rebels in the village of Ratyan, north of Aleppo. In early February, IS releases a video showing captured Jordanian pilot Moath Youssef al-Kasasbeh being burned alive leading to a series of retaliatory airstrikes by the Jordanian Air Force. Kurdish fighters reconquer villages near Tel Hamis in the northeast towards the end of the month, forcing an IS retreat. The jihadist group then launches an offensive in the west of the country, attacking the government-held Tadmur airbase in the Homs Governorate. In early March, Abu Homam al-Shami, military chief of the Nusra Front, is killed during regime airstrikes. However, the Nusra-led Jaish al-Fatah (Army of Conquest) captures the city of Idlib near the end of the month. Gains made by all sides fail to break the wider stalemate.

April–June

On the first day of April, IS takes large parts of Yarmouk refugee camp on the outskirts of Damascus after clashes with anti-Assad Palestinian militias. Two weeks later, the Kurdish People's Protection Units (YPG) and FSA take significant towns and territory near Kobane. However, IS responds to these losses by taking much of the town of al-Sukhnah in Homs province. In mid-May, the jihadist group captures the historic site of Palmyra from government troops, initiating a campaign of destruction that provokes international condemnation. It continues to push the regime back elsewhere, taking a number of towns and advancing within 35 kilometers of Homs. In another setback for pro-Assad forces, Jaish al-Fatah takes Ariha, the last regime-held town in Idlib province, threatening the government heartland of Latakia. In late June, IS resumes its efforts to retake Kobane, killing 146 civilians on the second day of the offensive in one of the conflict's largest massacres. An IS suicide bomber also kills 20 people in Hasakeh, the most important city in northeast Syria.

July–September

In early July, IS releases a video of a mass execution of 25 regime soldiers in Palmyra's amphitheater. Hezbollah and Syrian Army fighters enter the strategic town of Zabadani near the Beruit-Damascus highway, held by Nusra Front and other rebel groups. Regime forces make gains in pushing IS back from territory around Palmyra. The Syrian Air Force continues to make use of controversial barrel bombs, with a particularly large strike in mid-October killing 50 people in Douma, a suburb of Damascus under rebel control. Meanwhile, the regime loses territory to the Army of Conquest and FSA in the vital al-Ghab Plain. The area lies on the highway connecting the regime's heartland of Latakia with Aleppo, and control of it is crucial to government efforts to hold the latter. At the end of August, IS fighters attack the southern outskirts of Damascus. Rumors circulate of Russian airstrikes in early September, along with reports that Russian troops are conducting training drills inside regime territory. The government air force drops barrel bombs throughout September, causing many civilian deaths in Aleppo and Bosra. Airstrikes are also conducted against IS-held Raqqa. Later in the month, government forces recapture a number of villages around Hama. International tension increases, as France launches its first airstrikes against IS training camps and Russian President Vladimir Putin claims US support for rebels to be "illegal" according to UN resolutions. Shortly after, Russia begins its own campaign of airstrikes.

October–November
Egyptian President Abdel Fattah el-Sisi supports the Russian intervention. With Iranian and Russian support, the regime begins another offensive to retake Hama, but the FSA put up fierce resistance. However, the regime gains ground in Idlib province, capturing the villages of Atshan and Om Hartein. Relations between the United States and Russia worsen further, with a US government official claiming that Russian airstrikes are deliberately targeting CIA-trained rebels rather than IS, killing 150 to date.

In late October, international talks to resolve the crisis are held in Vienna. Notably, Iran is invited to participate for the first time. While agreeing on the need to defeat IS and bring regime and rebel representatives to the negotiating table, disagreement remains over the future of President Assad. Iran and Saudi Arabia reportedly clash, as do the United States and Russia. A week later, President Obama announces that US Special Forces will be sent to Syria in an "advisory" role. November sees a dramatic escalation in the international dimensions of the conflict, with a large-scale terror attack—believed to have been orchestrated by IS—killing 130 people in Paris. President Hollande vows to create a "grand coalition" to defeat IS. A few days later, the United Nations Security Council drafts a resolution committing them to destroying the group "by any means necessary." However, tension between international players rises as the Turkish Air Force shoots down a fighter jet in their airspace. Turkey claims it to be a legitimate act of defence; President Putin reacts by accusing Turkey of aiding IS and promising "serious consequences."

I.
ARAB SPRING, SYRIAN WINTER

A DOG IN LEBANON, AN OLD JOKE GOES, was so hungry, mangy and tired of civil war that he escaped to Syria. To the surprise of the other dogs, he returned a few months later. Seeing him better groomed and fatter than before, they asked whether the Syrians had been good to him. "Very good." "Did they feed and wash you?" "Yes." "Then why did you come back?" "I want to bark." It is impossible not to sympathize with Syrians' desire to be treated like adults. The Syrian regime is not alone, of course, among Middle East dictatorships in regarding its people as subjects rather than citizens. Under the portrait of the great dictator, petty tyrants grant some supplicants permits, demand bribes from others and abuse the rest. Syrians can identify with what Italians under Mussolini used to say: "The problem is not the big dictator. It is all the little dictators." Little dictators, though, thrive under the big dictator.

But all dictators are at risk from changed international circumstances, a spark (like a self-immolation in Tunisia) or the sudden realization that the regime is vulnerable. People in Syria have reasons to demand change, as they have in the past. But history has not been kind to Syria's desire for reform. During World War I, Arab nationalists in Damascus wanted to rid themselves of Ottoman rule. Ottoman officials could be corrupt and arbitrary, but they kept the peace, allowed the Syrians representation in the Istanbul parliament and put no restrictions on travel within the empire. The nationalists collaborated with Britain and France. They ended up with British and French colonialism, contrived borders, the expulsion of three-quarters of Palestine's population, insurrections and wars.

At independence in 1946, Syria had a parliamentary system, even if landlords, urban merchants, beys and pashas dominated it. Into the mix came the Arabian American Oil Company (Aramco), which had announced plans in 1945 to construct the Tapline oil conduit from Saudi Arabia to the Mediterranean. Three countries on the route—Saudi Arabia, Jordan and Lebanon—granted immediate permission. Syria's parliament, seeking better terms, delayed. The project stalled further when the Arab governments launched a war for which their colonially created armies (with the exception of Transjordan's) were unprepared. When they lost, demonstrations condemned the corruption that had deprived soldiers of adequate resources. In Damascus, the protesters forced the government to resign.

The United States embassy in Damascus seized the opportunity to win Syrian approval for Tapline. The Central Intelligence Agency's man, Stephen Meade, approached the army chief of staff, Colonel Husni Za'im, to arrange a coup. The Kurdish former Ottoman soldier took embassy money to foment an insurrection that justified his seizure of power in 1949. The embassy reported to Washington that "over 400 Commies [in] all parts of Syria have been arrested." Syria signed an agreement with Aramco in May and an armistice with Israel in July. Colonel Za'im antagonized sectors of society by raising taxes and attempting to give women the vote. Although he did not kill anyone, another colonel overthrew and executed him a month later. That colonel was himself eliminated by a third colonel. Thus began Syria's instability, with military coups as regular as changes of season. In the meantime, Colonel Za'im's suppression of the Communist Party produced, in the last free vote held in Syria, the election of the Arab world's first Communist member of parliament. The United States made two more major attempts in the 1950s to decide Syria's future—with Operation Straggle and Operation Wappen. Both failed. The era of chronic coups ended with the last one, Hafez al-Assad's, in November 1970. Syria enjoyed continuity, if not freedom, until the latest uprising was launched in 2011.

Revolutions elsewhere in the Middle East have also gone wrong, among them the Lebanese, Palestinian and Iranian. In 1975 young Lebanese, every bit as idealistic as their Syrian counterparts in 2011, began a revolution against corruption and pseudo-democracy. It produced a 15-year war, foreign occupation and devastation. The Palestinian revolution sold out, making the lives of the people it claimed to represent more wretched in the Israeli-occupied territories and in exile (most obviously, in Lebanon and Kuwait). The Iranian revolution, begun as a coalition of hope in 1978, led to a regime more brutal and corrupt than the one it replaced. Revolutions produce surprising outcomes, and those who start them must be prepared for the unintended consequences of success as much as for failure.

◆

In 1987, I traveled by land through what geographers called Greater Syria to write a book. I began in Alexandretta, the seaside northern province that France ceded to Turkey in 1939, on my way south through modern Syria to Lebanon. From there, my intended route went through Israel and Jordan. My destination was Aqaba, the first Turkish citadel of Greater Syria to surrender to the Arab revolt and Lawrence of Arabia in 1917. For various reasons, my journey was curtailed in Beirut in June 1987. (I returned to complete the trip and a second book in 2002.)

The ramble on foot and by bus and taxi gave me time to savor Syria in a way I couldn't as a journalist confronting daily deadlines. People loved to talk, linger over coffee and tea, play cards, and complain. One of the more interesting critics of President Hafez al-Assad's then 17-year-old Baathist regime was Hafiz Jemalli. Dr. Jemalli, a distinguished statesman and diplomat then in his 80s, had been a founder of the Baath Party. By 1987, he belonged to Syria's silent opposition.

"Everyone is afraid," he told me then. "I accepted to be a minister. Why? Because, if not, they put me in prison. Nobody has the courage to tell our president there is something wrong. Our president believes he is an inspired person, with some special relationship with God. If he is inspired, nothing is wrong. If there is some crisis, it is a plot, of Israel or America, but nothing to do with him, because he is inspired."

Many of the civilian members of the Baath Party, whose founders claimed to believe in secularism and democracy, deserted its ranks when the party took power in 1963. They rejected the militarization of the party, which kept power not through elections but by force of the arms of its members within the army. Among them was the father of Roulla Rouqbi, whom I met in 2012 at the hotel she manages in Damascus. Faissal Rouqbi had died a month earlier, which explained why the attractive 54-year-old was dressed in black. A vigorous supporter of the revolution that began in Syria the previous year, she believed it represented the same struggle her father waged against one-party military rule.

"I was questioned twice by the security forces," she told me in the hotel's coffee shop, which looks onto a busy downtown street. "They did it just to show me they know what I am doing and that they are here." She said that, because young dissidents gathered in her coffee shop with their computers, the police cut the hotel's Wi-Fi connection. Nonetheless, several young people were there discussing the rebellion, much as their forefathers did in the old cafés of the *souqs* that the French destroyed to put down their revolts, over strong Turkish coffee or, now, newly fashionable espresso.

Ms. Rouqbi detected a generational split in the conflict: "A lot of people here, nationalists of the old generation, are with the regime because they think it's against imperialism and the Zionist project." There was also an economic divide: "In Damascus, only the poor class is taking part. In Homs, all classes, all sects. It's really a revolution."

That was before the Arab Spring became the Syrian winter; before an uprising against dictatorship sparked by demonstrations against torture in the desert border town of Dera'a in 2011 degenerated into civil war. Syria had narrowly avoided civil conflict in 1982 and 1983. In 1982, President Hafez al-Assad was caught unawares by a Sunni Muslim uprising in the north. His younger brother, Rifaat, crushed the Muslim Brotherhood in the rebel movement's last stronghold in Hama, his special forces sparing no lives. Faced with an uprising of democrats in 2011, joined later by Sunni fundamentalists, Hafez's son and successor as president, Bashar, moved to crush unarmed demonstrators with the same ferocity. The violent suppression of peaceful dissent led some opponents to take up arms in defense of the right to protest and demand change. The armed men were a minority among dissidents who recoiled from the despoliation of their country that would necessarily accompany a violent uprising, yet they gained the ascendancy by the force of their actions and the international support they gained for their choice of the rifle over the banner.

As casualties mounted, advocates of a military solution dominated both the regime and the opposition camps. The center, inevitably, could not hold. Battles that had been limited to border zones, where rebels were easily supplied from Turkey, Jordan and Lebanon, spread to the rest of the country. Damascus and Aleppo, whose populations had for the most part either supported the regime or opposed it without resort to weapons, became theaters of bloody confrontation. The rebels, advised by intelligence officers from western countries working in Turkey and Lebanon, took outlying neighborhoods of Damascus. The regime, inevitably, used all the means at its disposal to drive them out and retake those areas. The next target of the rebels' strategy was Aleppo, where the pattern repeated itself: the rebels established themselves in the suburbs, residents fled and the regime returned with infantry, armor and airpower to "restore" order.

Many of the country's approximately 22 million people had a vested interest in the continuation of the Assad regime, even as others demand change. On Assad's side were the minorities who have done well under his and his father's rule since 1970, his own Alawite community, other quasi-Shiite groups, most of the Christians and parts of the Sunni merchant class. Against them stood fundamentalists, Syrians from every community whose families had felt the rough heel of injustice, and the young who were sickened by ways of governing that did not permit peaceful power transfers. But after living through two and a half years of violent war, many of the young idealists I met gathered in the café of Rulla Rouqbi's hotel when I returned in September 2013 were exhausted and discouraged, and the café itself nearly empty. "Stop the war. Stop the blood. The Syrian people are tired now," said Khaled Khalifa, author of the acclaimed Syrian novel *In Praise of Hatred*. He was fed up with the revolution he once longed for. "You can play revolution for some time," he said. "But not for a long time."

Many of the activists have been arrested. They include Professor Zaidoun al-Zoabi of the Arab Euro-

pean University and film festival director Orwa Nyarabia. Zoabi and Nyarabia were not tortured, although
Zoabi says he heard the screams of torture victims in
nearby cells. Interrogators may have spared them such
abuse because they belonged to what Graham Greene in
Our Man in Havana called the "non-torturable classes."
From prominent families, they were released and went
into exile. Others were not so fortunate. One former
protester told me, "I spent three days in jail, three days
of hell. I've gone back to my job and stay out of politics."
He fears the jihadists of the so-called Islamic State (IS)
more than the security forces who arrested him, and he
tries to avoid them both. "The demonstrations are fin-
ished," said a young woman whose activism has given
way to resignation. "That was the good time." The good
time ended almost as soon as it began.

If the revolutionaries are exhausted, so is the government; more tired still are the country's civilians, who
have borne the brunt of the suffering. According to the
UN nearly 200,000 people had been killed as of April
2014, probably an underestimate, while hundreds of
thousands more have been injured and maimed. Atrocities by both sides have become routine. On August 4,

2013, ISIS and other Islamist militias launched an offensive against Alawite villages in the hills above Latakia. A Human Rights Watch report, *You Can Still See Their Blood*, estimated that the rebels kidnapped more than 200 Alawite women and children before they withdrew 12 days later. Kenneth Roth, the head of Human Rights Watch, described how government forces indiscriminately attacked civilians with rockets, cluster bombs and other heavy weapons and used guns and knives to execute 248 civilians in a Sunni enclave that May. But he and his organization also condemned Islamists in the opposition for massacres and the ethnic cleansing of civilians "on a smaller scale":

> Human Rights Watch has collected the names of 190 civilians who were killed by opposition forces in their offensive on the villages, including 57 women and at least 18 children and 14 elderly men. . . . The evidence collected strongly suggests they were killed on the first day of the operation, August 4.

The Free Syrian Army, which distinguishes itself from the Islamists by claiming to represent Syrians of all sects, disassociated itself from the killings. Nonetheless, it has continued to cooperate with extreme Islamist jihadists in other operations against the government. Sectarian killings and hostage-taking—largely of Alawites and Christians—by the rebels terrify the minorities, but they do not threaten the regime. Instead, they force communities to turn to the regime for protection without bringing the war closer to a conclusion.

The UN's Human Rights Council, while condemning all factions, including the government, for atrocities, concluded a report on Syria, "There is no military solution to this conflict."

While armed struggle has indeed failed to end the war through outright victory, international diplomacy has done no better. The UN–Arab League initiative, led first by Kofi Annan, then by former Algerian foreign minister Lakhdar Brahimi and most recently by Staffan de Mistura, failed to break the impasse. While diplomats pursued talks about talks, Syrians died in the tens of thousands. "Children are paying the heaviest price in this war," reported United Nations Children's Fund

(UNICEF) Syrian Director Yusuf Abou Jelil in 2013. "Within Syria, four million children are directly affected. Two million are displaced in Syria. One million are on the front lines. One million are refugees." The escalation of suffering has reduced a country that fed itself before the war to living on international charity. Its medical and educational services, once among the best in the region, have been crippled. Children are suffering from malnutrition, and those in rebel areas have had difficulties receiving vaccines for polio, mumps, measles and rubella. At the end of October 2013, the World Health Organization confirmed an outbreak of polio among children in northeastern Syria. Dr. Annie Sparrow, a professor of public health at New York's Mount Sinai Hospital, described her conclusions from nearly 200 interviews with Syrian medical workers and civilians in the border regions of Lebanon and Turkey as follows:

> Over the past two and a half years, doctors, nurses, dentists, and pharmacists who provide treatment to civilians in contested areas have been arrested

and detained; paramedics have been tortured and used as human shields, ambulances have been targeted by snipers and missiles; medical facilities have been destroyed. . . . Five public hospitals have been taken over by the military, and there are no longer any left at all in the rebel-dominated cities of Idlib and Deir Ezzor. Fewer than forty ambulances in the country still function out of the original fleet of five hundred. . . . Now, more than 16,000 doctors have fled, and many of those left are in hiding. . . . At least thirty-six paramedics, in uniform on authorized missions, have been killed by Syrian military snipers or shot dead at checkpoints.

Emergency medical squads have been routinely prevented from evacuating not only wounded rebel fighters but also injured children and other civilians from rebel-held territory. Far from limiting the effects of the conflict on civilians, President Assad's counterinsurgency strategy has appeared to involve targeting the civilian population and medical facilities in rebel areas, in order to deprive the armed opposition of its support.

As of February 2014, more than 2.4 million Syrians were registered as refugees abroad, while Refugees International estimated that approximately 6.5 million have been internally displaced. Together, that's more than 40 percent of Syria's population. For many refugees, the rallying cries of the regime and of the armed opposition ring equally hollow. Some have been sheltered in tented camps in Turkey and Jordan, while others have found lodging within Lebanon with friends or relations or in disused buildings. Syrians, who earned an average of $300 a month when they had jobs, are paying rents of $100 a month or more to sleep in Bekaa Valley car parks or $500 for space above a garage. Others sleep rough and beg for sustenance in the streets of Lebanese cities. The exiled Syrians are learning what Palestinians have known since 1948: refugee existence is demeaning, cruel and crippling. Palestinian refugees themselves, 486,000 of whom are registered with the United Nations Relief and Works Agency (UNRWA) in nine camps in Syria, are suffering more now than at any time in their 64 stateless years.

A Syrian friend of mine had a summer villa perched in a hillside village between Damascus and the Lebanese border. Armed militants broke in and fired, from the roof, at an army post. Soldiers responded with mortars and machine-gun fire. The rebels ran away. No one won, and the house was wrecked. If a single image sums up the war in Syria, my friend's house does the job. Neither the troops nor the insurgents gave a damn about him or his house, and it's not clear how much either cares about the country.

◆

Syria has marked the fourth anniversary of a war that began with peaceful demonstrations. In mid-March 2011, the people of Dera'a protested against the torture of children arrested for writing anti-government graffiti. Their demands were not revolutionary: dismissal of Dera'a's governor and the trial of those responsible for torture. But for the people to demand, rather than beg, for anything from their government had violent consequences. The children's courage emboldened their elders to march through the streets of Damascus, Homs, Idlib and other cities to voice discontent, as they never had before. This was not a violent insurrection by religious obscurantists as in 1982, when the Muslim Brotherhood took up arms in Hama and Aleppo without consulting their inhabitants. Rather, this was a popular movement that was finding its way, learning from its mistakes and winning support.

As the protests spread, the regime responded, predictably, with gunfire, arrests and torture. But many of the demonstrators sought to continue peaceful opposition that would garner more and more public support, even at the risk of their lives. Other oppositionists believed that only weapons would bring change; they found outsiders willing to subsidize their methods. Regimes that were anything but models of democracy, namely Saudi Arabia and Qatar, poured in weapons and money. Turkey opened its border to arms, rebels and refugees. Clandestine training and logistical help came from the US, Britain and France. Protests turned to civil war. As in post-2003 Iraq, whose monuments and museums were ravaged, Syria had historic *souqs* and castles burned. Alawites and Sunnis, whose villages had coexisted through ages, turned on one another with Balkan ferocity. Christians were caught in the middle. Those who could do so fled.

The mosaic of cultures that made for Syria's richness is being lost.

The rebels calculated that, as in Libya, NATO would ensure their swift victory. The US decided that the regime was so unpopular that the rebels would overthrow it without NATO help. Both were wrong. Yet neither is taking the obvious alternative to the failed policy of violence: a negotiated settlement. Hillary Clinton, when she was US secretary of state, repeatedly said, as she did when Kofi Annan urged discussions between President Assad and his armed opponents, "Assad will still have to go." Her successor, John Kerry, took a more nuanced stance but did nothing to bring it about, while Britain and France devoted their energies to promoting arms transfers to the rebels. Russia and Iran have contributed primarily by sending weapons to the regime, and at least a half-dozen countries are meddling on the other side. Does anyone have the Syrians' well-being in mind?

Thomas Hardy, in his novel *The Woodlanders*, wrote of the knowledge required of anyone interfering with the lives of the people in his fictional Hintock:

> He must know all about those invisible ones of the days gone by, whose feet have traversed the fields which look so grey from his windows; recall whose creaking plough has turned those sods from time to time; whose hands planted the trees that form a crest to the opposite hill; whose horses and hounds have torn through that underwood; what birds affect that particular brake; what bygone domestic dramas of love, jealousy, revenge or disappointment have been enacted in the cottages, the mansions, the street or on the green.

Who in Washington, Moscow, Tehran, Riyadh or Doha has that understanding of Syria? Who among the politicians or dictators of those countries foresees the consequences of their inflaming Syrian passions with more weapons and money?

Hardy had in mind an outsider with no knowledge of Hintock's "bygone domestic dramas," a doctor named Edred Fitzpiers. Fitzpiers was treating the aged John South for an unnamed malady that appeared to be related to his fear of a tree growing outside his window. The doctor ordered: "The tree must be cut down, or I won't answer for his life." South woke the next morning and, seeing the hated tree gone, died. Fitzpiers said only, "D–d if my remedy hasn't killed him!"

II.
WITH FRIENDS LIKE THESE

SYRIANS USED TO TELL A JOKE ABOUT A survey that asked people of different nationalities, "What is your opinion of eating meat?" This was during the Cold War, so people in Poland answered, "What do you mean by 'meat'?" In Ethiopia, the response was, "What do you mean by 'eating'?" But in Syria, the universal response was, "What do you mean by 'what is your opinion'?"

Nothing much has changed, as Syrians confront the choice between a government they never voted for and a violent opposition dependent on foreign powers.

Think back to when this mess began, which was a long time before young Mohamed Bouazizi burned himself to death in Tunisia. It was about the time the British and the French decided to save the Arabs from the Ottoman Empire's oppression. "A man may find Naples or Palermo merely pretty," James Elroy Flecker, one-time British vice-consul in Beirut, wrote in October 1914, "but the deeper violet, the splendor and desolation of the Levant waters, is something that drives into the soul." A month later, Russia, Britain and France declared war on the Ottoman Empire in response to the Turkish fleet's foolhardy bombardment of Odessa and Sevastopol. Throughout Ottoman lands, where they had for centuries exercised considerable influence, consular staff from the Allied states departed their posts. Flecker died of tuberculosis barely a year later, aged 30, in the Swiss Alps, leaving behind a few dreamy letters and poems like "The Golden Journey to Samarkand." François Georges-Picot, a French consular officer in Beirut, also withdrew after war was declared. His legacy was a packet of letters implicating local notables in a conspiracy to detach Syria from the Ottoman Empire. Georges-Picot had lodged his papers at the American consulate and a dragoman there turned the evidence over to the new Turkish military governor, Jemal Pasha. Jemal had the 25 Christian and Muslim plotters tried for treason, found guilty and hanged, some in Damascus and the rest in Beirut on the site of what would subsequently be called, in their honor, Martyrs' Square.

The sultan's subjects who conspired with the French consul were naïve in colluding with a power that had no intention of granting them independence. All along, Britain and France, with imperial Russian complicity, had been operating under a 1916 secret agreement to divide the Ottoman Empire into British and French zones. The treaty, negotiated by Georges-Picot and Sir Mark Sykes, carved borders across a region that had not known them before and whose people did not want them. The new borders fragmented the region without settling the contradictions among competing nationalisms, and in 1917 Britain's Balfour Declaration added the complication of European Zionism. Britain's paramount concern was not what the Syrians wanted or needed but what *The Times* of August 21, 1919 called "the traditional rights and interests of France in Syria."

The inhabitants' own conceptions of what constituted the nation and its frontiers varied. Some believed in a Lebanese nation made up of Mount Lebanon and, possibly, the coastal cities and the Bekaa Valley. Others were Syrian nationalists, whose patrimony was Greater Syria, which meant all the territory south of Antioch as far as the Red Sea, including the future mini-states of Syria, Lebanon, Palestine and Transjordan. Most of the rest were Pan-Arabists, who sought the unity and independence of Arabic-speaking peoples from Morocco to Iraq. Between 1914 and 1918 all these nationalists united against the Ottomans, in opposition to the majority of their fellow subjects, who were either loyal to the empire or indifferent to nationalism's appeal. These differences would play themselves out in the decades following the Ottoman retreat. It's hard, however, to dispute the notion that the subjects of the empire were better off under the Ottomans than under the British, the French or the later regimes in Damascus, Beirut and Tel Aviv.

On the rare occasions when Syrians have been asked their opinion, their preferences were ignored. The most famous instance was in 1919, when Dr. Henry Churchill King and Charles R. Crane led a commission to assess what type of government the Arabs of the former Ottoman Empire desired. The British and French, having determined the region's fate in their secret agreement of 1916, refused to participate. So the Americans, in that innocent era before the discovery of oil in Arabia made them as avaricious as their imperial predecessors, set out on their own. From June 10 to July 21, 1919, the commission traveled from one end of Greater Syria to another, received 1,863 petitions and met 442 delegations from most ethnic and sectarian groups. More than 80 per cent of the petitioners demanded full independence and the continued unity of Syria, which then comprised today's Syria, Lebanon, Jordan and the areas that became Israel and Turkish Hatay (or Alexandretta).

The programs presented to the commission by all the Muslims and about two-thirds of the Christians of Syria were nationalistic; that is to say, they called for a United Syria under a democratic constitution, making no distinctions on the basis of religion. In response to repeated questions in many places, it was steadily affirmed by the Muslims that they had no desire whatever for Muslim privilege in the government, nor for political union with the Arabs of the Hejaz (now western Saudi Arabia), whom they felt to be in another state of civilization. Most inhabitants favored a constitutional monarchy under the Emir Feisal, who had led the Arab insurrection against the Ottomans. A year earlier, however, Feisal had learned from British General Edmund Allenby that his struggle, in which he had raised a force of nearly 30,000 men from all parts of Syria, had been futile.

T. E. Lawrence was present at the meeting on October 3, 1918, in newly conquered Damascus and later wrote of it in *Seven Pillars of Wisdom*: "Allenby gave me a telegram from the Foreign Office, recognizing to the Arabs the status of belligerents; and told me to translate it to the Emir: but none of us knew what it meant in English, let alone in Arabic: and Feisal, smiling through the tears which the welcome of his people had forced from him, put it aside to thank the Commander-in-Chief for the trust which had made him and his movement." More significantly, although Lawrence did not mention it in *Seven Pillars*, Allenby told Feisal that France would assume the government of Syria. The Arabs had risked their lives not for freedom but for British and French domination.

On July 24, 1920, French troops crossed from Beirut over Mount Lebanon to the Maysaloun Pass and defeated the cavalry of General Yusuf al-Azmeh. They expelled Feisal and imposed the so-called Mandate over little Syria and Greater Lebanon. Al Azmeh, the brave former Ottoman general who had been Feisal's minister of defense, gave his life to save the country from foreign domination, as did 1,200 Arab fighters. It was too late. Damascus fell to France, although the "natives" rebelled continually throughout the quarter-century of French rule.

Damascus was always at the heart of the rejection of disunity and foreign rule. In Damascus, wrote French Général Andréa in *La Révolte Druze et l'Insurrection de Damas, 1925–1926*, "the Arab heart beats more strongly than anywhere else." His observation preceded by 20 years Gamal Abdel Nasser's dictum that Syria was "the beating heart of Arabism," a phrase quoted from time to time by Syrian President Bashar al-Assad as posthumous benediction from the last, possibly the only, great Arab nationalist leader. Damascus was the capital of the first Arab empire, the Omayyad, in the seventh century. When its Sunni legions completed their conquest of Syria, they turned their might on Persia, a precedent not lost on the Shiite rulers of contemporary Iran. The Omayyads annexed all the territories from India west across North Africa to Spain, making theirs the most extensive imperium the world had known. Though illustrious, it had a duration of a mere 90 years. Thirteen centuries later, Damascus became capital of the first independent Arab kingdom to emerge from the defeated Ottoman Empire. Its tenure was a bare five months, from March 1920, when an elected Syrian Congress declared Sherif Feisal of the Hejaz its king, until French forces expelled him on July 28. Damascus's 7th-century empire and 20th-century kingdom, though vanished, inform the myths to which the city's inhabitants cling in turbulent times, as these are.

Soon after the French conquest of Damascus, *the Times* admitted that Feisal had "maintained public security throughout 1919 and 1920, along the desert edge of Syria, to a degree never attained by the Turks." Of course, this standard is comparative only, and his government was emphatically run by Syrians for Syrians. But he was a ruler of a country broken by four years of war, deprived of customs duties (that had been more than half the state's revenue) by the terms of the Sykes-Picot accord, distracted by the activities of his Turkish, French, British and Zionist neighbors and forbidden all foreign advice or technical assistance.

On August 7, 1920, *the Times* reminded its readers that Feisal's army had been in effect an adjunct of the British army during the war:

> The Arab army was equipped from the stores of the Egyptian Expeditionary Force in Cairo, and it was accompanied in the field by a small staff of British specialists in irregular war, who acted as advisers and as liaison between Feisal and Allenby.

As a British tool, Feisal's Arab army had to accept British occupation of Transjordan and Palestine, and French dominion in Syria and Lebanon.

France, having seized Syria, proceeded to divide it into four mini-states. Most Sunnis and Christians were Arab nationalists opposed to French rule. They refused to serve in the *Troupes Speciales du Levant* that became the Syrian Army, so the French recruited impoverished

Alawite peasants. The Alawite foothold in the armed forces was one legacy of that brutal 25 years of colonial rule, an inheritance that lies at the root of Syria's present crisis. The Alawites, whose daughters were mistreated as household servants in Damascus until recently, helped the French to crush nationalist rebellions in the 1920s. When the CIA sponsored the army coup that destroyed Syria's parliamentary democracy in 1949, the way was open for Alawite officers (whose survival over centuries of religious intolerance had required them to be master conspirators) to come to the fore in 1966.

When Bashar al Assad said that "Britain has played a famously unconstructive role in our region on different issues for decades," he was not, then, far off the mark. A country that, with France, imposed and modified the borders it drew across Ottoman Syria under the Sykes-Picot agreement carries historic baggage. A country that has done nothing since June 1967 to oppose Israel's occupation and annexation of Syria's Golan Heights has a way to go to prove its *bona fides* to a skeptical Syrian audience. And a country that, from the current rebellion's outset, predicted and sought the imminent downfall of the Damascus regime may find it hard to play the role of honest broker.

In 2012, a new armed force, calling itself the Free Syrian Army, seized many Syrian towns and parts of its main cities. Like Feisal's volunteers, its members were a mixture of idealists and opportunists.

There were other similarities: they received weapons, training and commands from outsiders; they had no idea what demands the foreign powers—among them the old imperialists Britain and France, as well as the United States, Turkey, Saudi Arabia and Qatar—would make of them if they should seize power in Damascus; and they did not know where their insurrection would lead the country.

When the rebellion's foreign patrons discuss Syria's fate, their own interests will inevitably prevail—as Britain's and France's did in 1920—over the desires of a "native government."

◆

Today Syrians are surrounded by more new-found friends than a lottery winner. Not since the old Soviet

Union signed all those "treaties of friendship" with everyone from Finland to Afghanistan has one country had so many new pals.

On the one side, Russia and Iran have supplied weapons, ammunition and diplomatic cover for President Assad. On the other, there is the Group of Friends of the Syrian People, a collection of 107 countries and organizations modeled on the Friends of Libya who cheer-led NATO's air war in that country. Where, you might ask, have these friends been hiding for the past 50 years? What were they doing in 1967 when Israel seized the Syrian Golan? What support did they send to more than 100,000 Syrian citizens when Israel demolished their villages and expelled them from their homes? What was their reaction to Israel's illegal annexation of the Golan in 1981? Have they taken a stand against the 30 settlements that Israel planted on property stolen from Syrians? Are they calling for sanctions against Israel until it withdraws from Syrian territory, dismantles its settlements and permits Syria's Golan citizens to return home?

Would it be churlish to suggest that Syria's friends want something from Syria for themselves?

You know the answers. So do the Syrians.

George W. Bush was eyeing Syria when he left the White House, and, as in so much else, the Obama administration has taken the policy further. On March 5, 2007, Seymour Hersh, whose American intelligence sources are second to none, wrote in *the New Yorker*:

> To undermine Iran, which is predominantly Shiite, the Bush administration has decided, in effect, to reconfigure its priorities in the Middle East. In Lebanon, the administration has co-operated with Saudi Arabia's government, which is Sunni, in clandestine operations that are intended to weaken Hezbollah, the Shiite organization that is backed by Iran. The US has also taken part in clandestine operations aimed at Iran and its ally Syria. A by-product of these activities has been the bolstering of Sunni extremist groups that espouse a militant vision of Islam and are hostile to America and sympathetic to Al Qaeda.

When Syria erupted in 2011, the US and Russia turned up with flame-throwers.

Four years on, a conflict that has screamed from the outset for a diplomatic settlement perpetuates itself with outside help, for outside interests. External support has not merely escalated the killing but, mirroring fratricidal struggles from Spain in 1936 to Yugoslavia in 1992, made it ever more personal and vicious. No hands are clean. No one, apart from the undertaker, is winning. Yet it goes on and on with each side certain of the justice of its cause.

Veteran Moroccan diplomat Mokhtar Lamani, who became the UN–Arab League representative on the ground in Syria in September 2012 and resigned two years later in frustration, has engaged with rebels and government officials across Syria. Comparing Syria to Iraq, where he served as Arab League representative from 2000 to 2007, Lamani said, "It's even worse here." Syria has become the venue of what he called "a proxy war" or wars: the United States versus Russia; the Sunni theocracies of Saudi Arabia and Qatar against the Shiite theocrats of Iran; and Turkey versus Arab nationalists over the attempted restoration of Turkey's pre–World War I dominance. The original demands for reform and justice of the peaceful protesters at the start of the uprising in 2011 are as forgotten as, two years and millions of deaths into the Great War, was Austria-Hungary's July 23, 1914, ultimatum to Serbia.

The CIA has been arming and guiding gunmen near the Turkish border, as it once did anti-Sandinista Contras along the Honduran-Nicaraguan frontier. To avoid Congressional scrutiny as it did in Nicaragua, the US turned again to Saudi Arabia. The British have run anti-Syrian government operations from Lebanon. France, my sources say, has played a similar role from both Turkey and Lebanon. Russia and Turkey still vie for influence in a country whose citizens hate them both.

If Syria's friends set out to destroy the country, they have done well. The war has reached the stage at which many on both sides no longer regard the others as human, let alone as citizens of a country in which all must coexist. Neighbor has turned against neighbor. People who thought of themselves in 2010 as Syrians have become Sunnis, Druze, Christians or Alawites. The introduction of chemical weapons, which have been alleged to have been used not only by the government but by the rebels as well, was only the most dramatic escalation by combatants who seek nothing short of the annihilation of the other side. The population that survives the violence is contending with famine, disease and exposure to the extremes of Syria's summers and winters.

While Syrians do most of the fighting and dying, both sides have welcomed foreigners into their ranks. Iranians and Lebanese Shiites reinforce the government army, while Sunni jihadists from more than 40 countries have become the revolt's shock troops. The latter are less concerned with majoritarian democracy than with deposing a president whose primary offenses they consider to be his membership in an Islamic sect, the Alawites, that they condemn as apostate, and his alliance with Shiite Iran. A Red Cross worker who, like Lamani, has worked on both sides of the barricades, said, "If there are secularist rebels, I haven't met them."

For outsiders whose own countries will not be the chessboard on which this game is played, war makes more political capital than the more subtle and difficult route of negotiation and compromise. Yet which is more likely to preserve Syria, its secularism, its economy and the healthy relations among its communities—civil war, as in Spain, Lebanon and Yugoslavia, or the example of Nelson Mandela meeting the enforcers of apartheid? When the British government and the Irish Republican Army swallowed pride and distaste to negotiate seriously, rather than win outright, the war in Northern Ireland ended.

The record of foreign military intervention is, to put it mildly, less impressive. Dissidents, journalists and mullahs who call for foreign forces to fight in Syria have only to look next door to Lebanon. During its long war, every foreign power that got involved burned its fingers and escalated violence for the Lebanese. The Palestine Liberation Organization (PLO) ostensibly responded to an appeal from Lebanon's Sunni Muslims for help in obtaining equality with the Christians. When the PLO left in 1982, their movement was badly wounded and even the Sunnis were glad to see it go. Syria intervened at various stages of the war on behalf of the Christians, the Palestinians and the Shiites. Its departure in April 2005 was welcomed by the vast majority of Lebanese. Israel came in 1982 promising to help the Christians. When it left in 2000, not even the Christians had a good word for them. As for the US's brief encounter with Lebanon in 1982-83, the less said, the better. Do the families of the 241 American service personnel killed in the suicide bombing of October 23, 1983, believe the price was worth paying?

◆

In October 2014, the militants of the self-proclaimed Islamic State in Iraq and Syria (ISIS) murdered another western captive, Alan Henning. Henning, like his fellow humanitarian worker David Haines, had gone to Syria out of compassion for its people in the midst of a vicious civil war. His sympathy and bravery did not matter to ISIS any more than the pleas for mercy by the Henning and Haines families. ISIS beheaded both men as it did the American journalists James Foley and David Sotloff and more recently American aid worker Abdul-Rahman Kassig. The western world appears to be powerless to protect any of these captives.

No one can be sure how many of the journalists and aid workers who have gone missing in rebel-held areas of Syria are in ISIS hands, but it is a fair bet that the Islamic State will carry out more executions as long as the war goes on. ISIS has not hesitated to behead Syrian, Iraqi and Lebanese civilians and captured soldiers. As with its burning alive of a young Jordanian Air Force pilot, Moaz al-Kasasbeh, it uses the public murders as propaganda to recruit jihadists rather than as a negotiating ploy. It has also enslaved, sold and raped hundreds, perhaps thousands, of Kurdish-speaking Yazidi women, as the United Nations Assistance Mission for Iraq (UNAMI) and the Office of the UN High Commissioner for Human Rights (OHCHR) have reported.

There is no magic formula to bring the hostages home, but Turkey has demonstrated that it can persuade ISIS to release captives. In September, ISIS set free the 49 Turkish hostages it kidnapped in Mosul on June 11, 2014. Turkey denied that it paid ransom, which may or may not be true. While it attributed the release to a "rescue operation," there was no evidence of a struggle, which means the "rescue" was more likely diplomatic than military. Turkey's past support for Islamic fundamentalists in Syria has given it leverage that made ransom irrelevant, because Turkey holds the power to deny ISIS access to arms, fighters and equipment from its territory across the border into Syria and Iraq.

When I was in northern Syria in September 2014, Armenian villagers told me they had seen Turkish military vehicles bringing Islamist fighters to the border to conquer Armenian villages in the area of Kessab last March. Turkey is not the only enabler of the Islamist fundamentalists who have kidnapped and murdered Syrians, Iraqis and Westerners since 2011. Two other Middle East allies of the United States and Britain, namely Qatar and Saudi Arabia, funded the groups that became ISIS throughout the Syria rebellion against President Assad.

American Vice President Joe Biden admitted as much to Harvard University's John F. Kennedy Forum:

> And what my constant cry was that our biggest problem is our allies—our allies in the region were our largest problem in Syria. The Turks were great friends—and I have the greatest relationship with [Turkish President Recep Tayyip] Erdogan, which I just spent a lot of time with—the Saudis, the Emiratis, etc. What were they doing? They were so determined to take down Assad and essentially have a proxy Sunni-Shia war, what did they do? They poured hundreds of millions of dollars and tens, thousands of

tons of weapons into anyone who would fight against Assad except that the people who were being supplied were al-Nusra and al-Qaeda and the extremist elements of jihadis coming from other parts of the world.

What Biden neglected to say was that America's allies conducted that policy with the knowledge of the United States, which did nothing to stop it. The weapons supplied to the fanatics were manufactured in the US, and American intelligence in Turkey knew which rebels Turkey, Qatar and Saudi Arabia were assisting. Moreover, the moving forces within ISIS, including its mercurial leader Abu Bakr al-Baghdadi, were graduates of the American prison system in Iraq, where previously non-political Sunni Muslims became radicals.

ISIS's brutal rise has complicated the alignment of foreign forces in Syria. In 2014, the United States reversed its policy from threatening to bomb the Syrian regime to bombing its enemies. This gave the regime hope. It saw that not only would it survive, but that it would become, however covertly, a partner of the nations that had worked most assiduously to remove it. I was in Syria just before the US began bombing

ISIS-held towns, with the predictable civilian casualties and targets that turned out to be grain silos and private houses, and Syrian officials were anticipating American involvement with satisfaction.

Contacts with the US had been underway at least since June 20, when Syrian presidential adviser Bouthaina Shaaban met former US President Jimmy Carter and former Assistant Secretary of State for Near Eastern Affairs Jeffrey Feltman in Oslo. Feltman was attending a conference as a newly appointed UN official, but he still had his State Department connections. Officials present at his meeting with Dr. Shaaban recounted a conversation in which Feltman told her, "We know President Assad is going to stay, but you know what President Obama said. So, how can we solve the problem?" Having said for four years that Assad must go, Obama has yet to explain why Assad can, for the time being, stay. This change would not be unusual for an American president, since the recurring theme in US–Syria relations throughout the Assad era has been one of hostility followed by cooperation—that is, cooperation when both sides needed it.

During the early years of Hafez al-Assad's rule, Richard Nixon and Henry Kissinger refused all dealings with the ostensibly pro-Soviet ruler. The October 1973 war, launched by Egypt and Syria to regain territories Israel occupied in 1967, put an end to that. Kissinger flew to Damascus in December 1973 and wrote later:

> Withal, I developed a high regard for Assad. In the Syrian context he was moderate indeed. He leaned toward the Soviets as the source of his military equipment. But he was far from being a Soviet stooge. He had a first-class mind allied to a wicked sense of humor.

The US opened an embassy in Damascus in 1974 and enjoyed a brief honeymoon with Assad *père*, until his meddling in Lebanon made him *persona non grata* again in Washington. A near victory by Palestinian commandos in Lebanon's civil war in 1976 prompted Kissinger to ask Assad to send his army into Lebanon to control the Palestine Liberation Organization and save Lebanon's Christians.

By 1982, the US was again fed up with Assad for giving aid to Yasser Arafat. That turned out to be disastrous for Arafat. Syrian tolerance of his actions only worsened his situation and that of his people as Palestinian commandos had a part in dividing and ruining Lebanon. Ronald Reagan let the Israelis drive Assad's army out of most of Lebanon. A few years later, when Hezbollah was making life unbearable in West Beirut and Westerners were easy pickings for kidnappers, the first Bush administration invited Syria back into the region that its army had evacuated in 1982. This was followed by another freeze in relations that ended when Bush and his secretary of state, James Baker, asked Syria to take part in the war to expel Iraq from Kuwait. Assad obliged, making him a temporary hero at the White House if something of a pariah to those of his citizens who were Arab nationalists.

After September 11, the US rendered terrorism suspects to Syria for torture. That relationship ended with the assassination of former Lebanese Prime Minister Rafic Hariri in 2005 and Syria's humiliating withdrawal from Lebanon after it was accused of conspiring against Hariri. If his father survived the ups and downs of that seesaw, young Bashar, who succeeded him in 2000, has a good chance of riding out a rebellion that has become, as he had prematurely claimed at its inception, an uprising of fanatics and terrorists who want to take Syria into a dark age.

As Bashar's prospects improve with each American sortie against his enemies in the east of the country, Damascus and the populous towns to the north have been enjoying a respite of sorts from war. The Syrian Ministry of Education reported that, of the 22,000 schools in the country, more than 17,000 of them reopened on time in the middle of September 2014. Needless to say, almost all of the functioning schools were in government held areas. The *souqs* in the old city of Damascus, unlike their more extensive and now destroyed counterparts in Aleppo, have remained open. Shops selling meat, vegetables, spices and other basic items to the local population have thrived, although the tourist boutiques in and around the famous Souq Hamadiyeh had no customers apart from UN workers and a few diplomats. At night, restaurants in most neighborhoods were on my many visits, if not full, nearly so. Everything from wine to grilled chicken is plentiful, albeit at prices higher than before the war. Traffic remains heavy, although somewhat less obstructed since June 2014 when the government felt confident enough to remove many of its checkpoints. Electricity has been intermittent, and those who can afford private generators relied on them in the off-hours.

In the old city of Damascus, where I stayed in September in an Ottoman palace converted into a hotel, I heard each morning at eight the roar of Syrian warplanes. They ran bombing missions on the suburb of Jobar, not more than a few hundred yards from the old city's walls. Most of Jobar's inhabitants fled long ago, and its buildings have dissolved to rubble under relentless shelling. The rebels are said to be safe underground in tunnels that they or their prisoners have dug over the past two years. They fire the occasional mortar, which the Damascenes ignore. People in the city refuse to see and hear the violence in their suburbs, much as Beverly Hills ignored riots in Watts in 1965 and 1992. It becomes easy to pretend there is no war, unless a bomb falls too close or kills someone you know. One morning as I was driving through the upscale Abu Rummaneh quarter, a rebel mortar shell whistled overhead, hit a fuel storage tank and sent black smoke soaring into the sky. Yet the shoppers around the corner went on as if nothing happened.

Jobar was one of the few outlying areas of the capital still in rebel hands in late 2014, but the government has dealt more successfully with the others. It has recaptured some, like Mleiha on August 14. In others, a UN official said, the strategy has been subtler. Commanders from the warring sides make local agreements not to fight one another. "Local agreements for them are just stages of their military strategy," said a United Nations official involved in talks between the two sides. "Fragment areas. Isolate them. Besiege them, until the people understand that they are not going to win the war and are going to negotiate. The opposition calls this a policy of kneel or starve. . . . The government uses the term 'reconciliation.' We call it 'surrender.'"

A young Druze friend, who like the rest of his community has struggled not to take sides, said, "People are exhausted. Even those who fought the regime are moving toward reconciliation." It is hard to blame them, when more than 200,000 Syrians have died and another nine million have become refugees inside and outside their country in a war that has, to date, achieved nothing except death and destruction.

"It's a lot quieter in Damascus," admitted a UN aid worker, "but there are other places that are on fire." Yet the fire is burning far to the north and east of Damascus, many miles from the heartland of populated Syria. The roads west to Lebanon and north from Damascus to Homs look as if central Damascus has become a green zone that is contiguous with the regions the regime considers vital to its survival. The first sight as I drove on the highway north out of the capital in the summer of 2014 was the district of Harasta, destroyed and mostly deserted. Then came Adra, an industrial town that was brutally captured in 2013 by Islamists who massacred its Alawite inhabitants. Shortly after I drove past, the government took it back and invited its industrial workers to return.

Farther north, the highway crosses open land of farms and peasant hamlets. In 2013, the route there was not safe. Bandits and rebels alike set up flying checkpoints to demand money or cars and to kidnap those who looked prosperous enough to afford ransom. It was a no-go zone for minority sects like the Alawites, Ismailis, and Christians, as well as for visiting Westerners. A year later, the atmosphere had changed. The rebels in Homs, said in 2011 to be the cradle of the revolution, surrendered their positions to the government and left with their light weapons in May 2014. Only the district of Al Wa'er, about a mile from the old city, remained in rebel hands and under regime siege. There was a tense and regularly violated truce, but the city had been pacified. Some civilians returned home, even to houses that needed rebuilding after four years of fighting. Christians fleeing from areas taken by ISIS and the Islamic Front groups found temporary refuge in an Armenian church in the city, and local aid organizations helped people of all sects.

The road west from Homs toward the sea was by mid-2014 safe for anyone not allied to the rebels. The famed Krak des Chevaliers Crusader fortress, from which rebels were able to shell the highway and nearby villages, had reverted to the government. So had the towns of Qosair and Qalamoun, which the rebels needed to keep their lines of supply open to Lebanon. The road runs through fields where the apple harvest has begun and the olives would soon be collected. The coastal city of Tartous was buzzing with life, as if there had never been a war. The ferry to Arwad Island, where families go for lunch, was running every 20 minutes.

Farther north, the port of Latakia has suffered shelling only on the rare occasions that rebels took positions in the Alawite hills above it until the army quickly pushed them back. It may sound odd to anyone outside Syria who has followed the conflict, but the beach in front of my hotel in Latakia was filled with families swimming and not a few women in bikinis.

There was fear, however, that a major onslaught by ISIS and similar jihadist groups would put an end to these pockets of ordinary life. It is hard for Syrians to accept that the countries in the Gulf and elsewhere that supported ISIS with arms, financing and fighters are now signing up to an American coalition to bring it down. Yet ISIS may have gone too far, even for its backers. The caliphate that it declared in parts of Syria and Iraq struck a strong chord with Islamist fanatics in Saudi Arabia, Qatar, Turkey and other states that had facilitated the group's rapid and rabid expansion. These states must fear that the movement they brought to Syria will come to haunt them. "It's like the lion tamer," an Arab diplomat in Damascus told me. "He feeds and trains the lion, but the lion might kill him at the right moment."

III.
A SHATTERED MOSAIC

NO EVENT LOOMS LARGER IN MODERN Syrian history than the Great Syrian Revolt of 1925. Syrians recall it as a nationalist revolution against foreign occupation, while to French Général Andréa, in his memoir of its suppression, "*C'est du banditisme tout pur.*" That insurrection erupted unexpectedly, like the rebellion against President Bashar al-Assad in March 2011, during a drought in the Hauran, a plateau rich in wheat and vines beside a rugged basalt mountain south of Damascus. Similarities between the rebellions of 1925 and 2011 are many. Both started with petitions and non-violent demonstrations over discontent with local governors. Both caught the authorities unawares. Both spread to Homs before engulfing the rest of the country. Both received weapons from Turkey, Saudi

Arabia and Jordan. Both comprised rival factions of secularists and Islamists, democrats and theocrats, tribesmen and city sophisticates, Syrians and outsiders. Both, despite provoking bombardment from airplanes and heavy artillery, enjoyed initial success. The first was defeated, and the second—despite the gains made by the fundamentalist Islamic State in Iraq and Syria (ISIS)—is losing as well.

Every Syrian government since the final departure of the French Army on April 17, 1946, has claimed to incarnate the spirit of the Great Revolt. Yet each Syrian government found itself in the position of the French, governing and modernizing a country that tended to resist both projects. France's High Commissioners, like their indigenous successors, failed to absorb the greatest lesson of four centuries of Ottoman trial and error in Syria: to govern well, govern little. The Turks, while introducing haphazard and occasional reforms and hanging fomenters of sectarian warfare, barely tampered with the structure of governance they inherited from Rome, Byzantium and the Omayyads. That is to say, they left the tribes and sects to their local chiefs. The French, as well as the assorted civilian and military regimes that followed in their wake, were more ambitious.

Governing Syria has never been easy, as the commanders of punitive expeditions from Titus to the Ottomans' last general could attest. Two years into the French League of Nations Mandate over Syria and Lebanon, a Scottish traveler, Helen Cameron Gordon, toured the country and later described conditions that would daunt any sovereign, foreign or local. She wrote:

> Her inhabitants are made up of at least a dozen different races, mainly Asiatic; and worse still, of about thirty religious sects, all suspicious and jealous of each other.

> Amongst Christians alone, there are seventeen high dignitaries with the title of Patriarch, and other leaders politically minded and steeped in intrigue: Moslems, Druses, Ismaelites, Nosairis [Alawites], Yessides and various sub sects too numerous to mention. Influence, that is pernicious, is brought to bear upon them from outside, which they are themselves unequal to combat, and sometimes prone to pay too

much attention. Is it to be wondered that amongst officers of the Army of the Levant, it has become proverbial that peace is only in the shadow of their bayonets and within the radius of their machine-guns?

Sir Mark Sykes, in his *Dar Ul-Islam: A Record of a Journey through Ten of the Asiatic Provinces of Turkey* (1904), similarly observed:

> The population of Syria is so inharmonious a gathering of widely different races in blood, in creed, and in custom, that government is both difficult and dangerous.

Yet the history of Syria's fragile mosaic is one of surprising coexistence and tolerance. Take Ahmad Badreddine Hassoun, who recounted with fondness a drive he made with his wife from Montreal via Toronto to New York in 1994. Somewhere past Niagara Falls, the couple stopped at a McDonald's. All the seats were taken. "I was dressed like this," Hassoun said, pulling at the lapel of his robes, "and my wife was in *hijab*." An American man, aged about 65, got up and offered them his table.

When Hassoun declined, the man insisted, "I'm an American, and I can go home and eat. You are my guest."

The gesture impressed Hassoun, who became grand mufti, or chief Sunni Muslim religious scholar, of Syria 11 years later: "A good human being is a good human being. I don't know if that man was Jewish, Christian or Muslim." Mufti Hassoun belies the stereotype of the Muslim clergyman. He has preached in the Christian churches of Aleppo, Syria's second city, and he has invited bishops to speak in his mosque. His official interpreter is an Armenian Christian. "I am the mufti for all of Syria, for Muslims, Christians and non-believers," he says, an ecumenical sentiment placing him at odds with more fundamentalist colleagues among the religious scholars known as the *ulema*.

The contrast with many other Sunni Muslim clergymen is stark. Another Syrian mullah, Sheikh Adnan al-Arour, broadcasts regularly from Saudi Arabia with a different message: "The problem is actually with some minorities and sects that support the regime . . . and I mention in particular the Alawite sect. We will never harm any one of them who stood neutral, but those who stood against us, I swear by Allah, we will grind them and feed them to the dogs." Another Sunni preacher, the Egyptian Sheikh Mohammad al-Zughbey, went further: "Allah! Kill that dirty small sect [the Alawites]. Allah! Destroy them. Allah! They are the Jews' agents. Kill them all ... It is a holy *jihad*."

"I don't believe in holy or sacred wars or places," Hassoun said. "The human being is sacred, whether Muslim, Christian, Jewish or non-believer. Defend his rights as if you are defending the holy books." His tolerance and acceptance of the secular state in Syria have earned the mufti condemnation as a mouthpiece for a repressive regime and threats from Salafist Muslims, whose interpretation of Islam excludes tolerance of atheists, Christians and Shiites. Yet the mufti's views are not atypical in Syria, where Islam and Christianity have coexisted for 15 centuries, and which the Greek poet Meleager of Gadara called, in the first century BC, "one country which is the whole world."

The world of communities dwelling in Syria includes its Sunni Muslim Arab majority alongside a multitude of minorities: Sunni Kurds; Armenian and Arab Christians of Catholic, Orthodox and Protestant denominations; Assyrians; Circassians;

Kurdish Yazidis, with their roots in the teachings of Zoroaster; and the quasi-Shiite Muslim sects of Druze, Ismailis and Alawites. The Syrian population included a few thousand Jews, descendants of ancient communities, until 1992. The country is one of the few places where Aramaic, the regional lingua franca at the time of Christ, is still spoken. In one Aramaic-speaking village, Maalula, it was not unusual for Muslim women to pray with Christians for the births of healthy children at the convent of Saint Takla.

During centuries of productive coexistence, there were only two outbreaks of sectarian conflict that resulted in massacres. Both took place in the mid-19th century, when Christians were accumulating wealth thanks to their association with Christian businessmen from Europe. In the first, a minor incident in Aleppo in 1850 sparked a Muslim massacre of Christians and the burning of several churches. No more than a dozen Christians were killed, but many more lost property to looters and vandals. Ten years later, a similar incident in Damascus led to the massacre of 11,000 Christians. Nineteenth-century Christians were close to the Europeans who came to dominate the country's economic life, and today's Christians and Alawites are seen as too close to a regime that many Sunni Muslims detest as much as their ancestors did the Europeans. Those who have done well out of 42 years of Assad family rule now fear the revolution may end with that bloody history repeating itself.

◆

France's Armée du Levant engaged in nearly continuous counterinsurgency from the moment it invaded Syria. The Alawite minority under Salih al-Ali fought the French for a year in the northwest, as did a largely Sunni force led by a Kurdish former Ottoman officer, Ibrahim Hananu, around Aleppo. In the Hauran and its mountain, alternately called Jabal Hauran and Jabal Druze, the French skirmished often with King Feisal's former partisans, who made cross-border raids from his brother Abdallah's new principality of Transjordan. Many Druze fought them until 1922, when France granted a "Druze Charter of Independence" with local autonomy and an elected Druze *Majlis* or Council. By the time Général Maurice Sarrail, France's third High

Commissioner in four years, disembarked in Beirut on January 2, 1925, Syria had been subdued.

Nowhere appeared quieter than the formerly turbulent Druze region in the highlands of the Hauran. The *Majlis* had even chosen a French officer, Captain Gabriel Carbillet, as governor in July 1923, when they could not agree on a Druze candidate. Carbillet was a man of the Left, anti-clerical and a Freemason, who determined to bring *égalité* to the Druze by enfeebling their aristocracy. Joyce Laverty Miller wrote in the *International Journal of Middle East Studies* in 1977:

> Carbillet proved to be an ambitious and zealous reformer. In the course of a year, he opened twenty-three new schools, equalized the civil laws, opened a court of appeals at al-Suwaida (the capital city of Jabal-Druze), constructed an extensive system of irrigation, built roads, disarmed the population, and used the forced labor of prisoners and peasants.

Among his achievements was to bring running water for the first time to Suwaida. He also built five museums, but his use of conscripted *corvée* labor caused resentment.

So too did his collective punishment of Druze peasants and sheikhs alike, whom he forced to break rocks under the Syrian sun. Like George W. Bush's neoconservative true believers in occupied Iraq, Carbillet had a vision. He asked, "Should I leave these chiefs to continue their oppression of a people who dream of liberty?"

France introduced something new into Syrian life, something that lingers to this day. In his book *Syria and Lebanon Under French Mandate*, Stephen Hemsley Longrigg writes, "Rigid control of personal movement was established. The use of schoolmasters as informers was everywhere practiced. Punishments, for offenses sometimes trivial, were arbitrary and even capricious. The sensitiveness of Druze pride was repeatedly offended."

Like the Trojan War, the Great Syrian Revolt of 1925 resulted from breaches of hospitality. As Paris stole his host's wife, functionaries from Third Republic Paris made a gross *faux pas* in the village of Qraya on July 7, 1922. Armed soldiers broke into the house of Sultan Pasha al-Atrash, who was away, to arrest a Shiite named Adham Kanjar on charges of attempting to assassinate the High Commissioner, Général Henri Gouraud.

Al-Atrash, a 31-year-old hotspur with penetrating azure eyes and formidable moustaches, a visual embodiment of the noble Druze warrior, had served in the Ottoman Army before defecting in 1918 to Sherif Feisal and the British. When the absent al-Atrash discovered the French had desecrated his house, he demanded Kanjar's return. The French refused. Al-Atrash, as a notable whose prestige depended on his power to protect others, attacked a train he mistakenly believed to be carrying the prisoner to Damascus. The French retaliated by demolishing his house and ordering his capture. He fled, returning a year later under an amnesty.

The *Observer*, in an article on August 9, 1925, sub-headed "Quarrel with a Young Governor," traced the revolt's spark to a subsequent violation of the Druze code of hospitality. The "young governor," Captain Carbillet, had overseen the construction of the first hotel in the Druze capital at Suwaida and required travelers to lodge there rather than as guests in private houses. The *Observer* wrote:

[Nesib] al-Atrash Bey pleaded that the century-old traditions of hospitality could not thus be broken, and finally roundly suggested that the Governor was financially interested in the fortunes of the hotel, and refused to yield, whereupon the notables guilty of having opened their houses to travelers were seized and sent to break stones on the roads.

The al-Atrash family appealed to the senior French official in Syria, newly arrived High Commissioner Sarrail, in February 1925. Sarrail, like Carbillet in a minority among French officers as a staunch republican and progressive, declined to receive the 40-man delegation. When they persisted, he arrested their leaders. Nesib Bey al-Atrash was reported to have told the French, "Very well. Rifles will speak." The arrested Druze were sent to France's new prison in the desert at Palmyra, where Sarrail's secretary, Paul Coblentz, admitted that treatment "was certainly not always comparable with the methods used in similar cases in Europe."

In March 1925, Captain Carbillet went to France on leave. A more conservative officer, Captain Antoine Raynaud, filled in for him. Raynaud's light-handed governance made him popular, especially among the landlords. When a French parliamentarian, Auguste Brunet of the

Radical Party, came to Beirut on what a later era would call a fact-finding mission, Druze delegates presented him with a petition calling on France to make Raynaud's appointment permanent. Brunet ignored the petition, and Sarrail once again rebuffed their deputation.

The Druze graduated from polite petitions to public protest. Their newly formed Patriotic Club staged a demonstration on the morning of July 3 in front of the *Majlis* in Suwaida, where Captain Raynaud was presiding over a council session. About 400 Druze horsemen shouted demands, chanted war songs and carried weapons, while refraining from violence. When French-officered gendarmes dispersed them, though, shots were exchanged between one Druze leader, Hussein Murshid, and French Lieutenant Maurel. Neither man was hit, and the Druze offered an immediate apology. Captain Raynaud, despite the fact that the demonstrators' goal was to retain him as governor, commanded the Druze to pay a large fine and turn over 20 young men for detention. He also ordered the immediate demolition of the house of Hussein Murshid. The Druze religious sheikhs intervened to prevent bloodshed, agreeing that the community would pay the fine and turn over the young men. But destruction of a Druze house was not acceptable.

French troops appeared at Murshid's house to tear it down, but Sultan al-Atrash, hundreds of mounted men and neighbors with rifles forced them to withdraw. Raynaud sent a warning to High Commissioner Sarrail that discontent was leading inevitably to revolution. Sarrail dismissed Raynaud and assigned an officer from the Intelligence Corps, Major Tommy Martin, to fill his post pending Carbillet's return. Sarrail summoned five Druze chiefs, including Sultan al-Atrash, to Damascus. Fearing a trap, Sultan declined. He was not surprised when Sarrail arrested the others at their Damascus hotel and sent them to Palmyra.

Up to that time, the Druze had not demanded an end to the French Mandate, any more than Dera'a's demonstrators in early March 2011 initially sought to depose Bashar al-Assad. Their request for one French officer to replace another implied recognition of the Mandate. Similarly, the Dera'a protesters' call in 2011 for the dismissal of a governor who had crossed a line by torturing children acknowledged the president's authority to replace local officials who violated the law and trampled on their dignity. When the rulers refused to listen, the people's horizons expanded to a future in which they would choose new rulers.

Captain Carbillet returned from leave on July 19, but Sarrail did not restore him as governor. The governorship had ceased to be the issue, just as Bashar al-Assad's belated dismissal of Dera'a's governor, his cousin Faisal Kalthum, came too late to pacify the rebellion against his rule. The Druze and their allies, including many Sunni Muslims and a few Christians, demanded nothing less than France's expulsion and self-determination in a unified Syria.

On the day of Carbillet's return, two French reconnaissance planes spotted Sultan al-Atrash's growing insurgent band in the village of Urman. The Druze fired at the planes, downing one and capturing its two pilots. This became the date on which the Great Syrian Revolt is said to have begun. Michael Provence writes in his excellent history, *The Great Syrian Revolt and the Rise of Arab Nationalism*, "Neither rebel leaders nor the mandate authorities had a clear conception of the direction and seriousness of the uprising at this early point." Nonetheless, both sides escalated the violence.

The next day, Major Martin sent a force of about 200 French and colonial troops under a Captain Normand to retrieve the two pilots and crush what appeared to be a local disturbance. Normand bivouacked on July 21 beside a village halfway between Salkhad and Suwaida, where Sultan al-Atrash's envoys asked him to return to Suwaida for negotiations to end the fighting. Normand declined. During the battle that followed, Sultan al-Atrash's Druze and bedouin warriors destroyed Normand's force in about 30 minutes. A few stragglers made their way back to the garrison at Suwaida, which al-Atrash attacked the next day, laying siege to the French in the old citadel.

The destruction of the Normand column galvanized latent opposition to the French in Syria. Young men from Damascus joined the colors, as did Arab patriots from the recently created neighboring countries. Abdel-Aziz ibn Saud, who with his Wahhabi followers ruled the Nejd desert and had recently conquered Mecca and Medina from Britain's Hashemite allies, sent arms and men. Mustapha Kemal Pasha, the Turkish leader who had his own dispute with France over

Turkey's border with Syria, supported the rebels in the north. The French in turn armed Armenian refugees, barely recovered from massacres by Muslim Turks, as well as minority Circassians and Arab Christians. The rebels cut French communications, severing rail and telegraph lines at different times to Lebanon, Iraq and Transjordan.

To quell the uprising, Sarrail dispatched Général Roger Michaud, the Armée du Levant's commander, from Beirut to Damascus. Michaud led a large force south toward the Druze capital to relieve his besieged countrymen. On August 2, when his force rested about 12 kilometers short of Suwaida, Sultan al-Atrash attacked with 500 Druze and bedouin horsemen. The French drove them back, but, running short of water, began a withdrawal north the next day. Al-Atrash attacked again with greater force, annihilating the French column. Michaud's second-in-command, Major Jean Aujac, committed suicide in the field. Al-Atrash's men collected more than 2,000 rifles, as well as machine guns and artillery pieces, from the dead Frenchmen. Reuters reported, "The French have evacuated Southern Hauran."

French Foreign Minister Aristide Briand nonetheless declared that the situation in Syria was not
dangerous. France faced a greater threat in its Morocco
Protectorate, where insurgents from the Rif Mountain
were humiliating the armies of both France and Spain.
Moroccan success inspired the Syrians, much as the
downfall of the dictators in Tunisia, Egypt and Libya
would 90 years later. But the rebellions in Morocco and
Syria had far to go.

Unrest spread immediately to Homs, where
so-called "bandits" attacked outlying French positions and closed roads. The nationalist elite in
Damascus, who had remained quiet, were forced to
support the rebellion or stand accused of treason.
On August 23, al-Atrash requested negotiations with
Sarrail through his old friend Captain Raynaud. Just
as Sarrail had invited Druze leaders to Damascus as
a ruse to arrest them, al-Atrash's offer was a cover for
an assault on Damascus. On August 24, more than
a thousand men from Jabal Druze, the Hauran and
the desert mustered on the city outskirts. Arguments
among their leaders over strategy delayed their
advance, giving French planes time to locate and

strafe them. North African cavalry then drove them south.

Muslim soldiers from Algeria and Senegal began deserting the French army to join the rebels. So did local levies in France's Syrian Legion, including the Legion's commander in Hama, Fawzi al-Qawuqji, with all his men. The mutineers held Hama for two days, until ferocious French bombardment of the ancient *souqs* and residential quarters forced the town's notables to beg Qawuqji to spare the city by withdrawing.

As over the past four years, some rebel leaders claimed to speak for all Syrians—Arab Sunni Muslims, the various Shia sects and Christians. But not all the participants shared that universal vision. In 1925, some raised the flag of *jihad* and attacked the Christian town of Maalula. One of the revolt's more able leaders, Said al 'As, wrote:

> This work was not legitimate and the revolt was exposed to doubt by their attack and their hostility against Maalula which alienated the hearts of the Christian sons of the one nation, our brothers in nationalism and the homeland.

As the nationalists regretted the assault on Maalula in 1925, their descendants condemned the jihadist assault on the same Christian town in 2013. Yet the effect of both was the same: to drive Christians out of a country where they have lived since the time of Christ or to force them into the arms of the regime, French then and Baathist now.

By early October, the rebels had the initiative, forcing the French to confront them at times and places of their choosing. Their next target was Damascus, which they entered on October 18. Typical of the disorganization within rebel ranks, the local commander, Hassan al-Kharrat, invaded the city before Fawzi al-Qawuqji's mutineers and Sultan al-Atrash's Druze-bedouin cavalry arrived. Entering the Shaghur quarter, Kharrat shouted, "Rise up, your brothers the Druze are here!" Most Damascenes, like their descendants in this century, did not rise up.

As his forces lost control of Damascus, High Commissioner Sarrail declared martial law and commanded the summary execution of Syrians found with weapons. French tanks raced through the *souqs*, wrote *the Times*, "at terrifying speed, firing to the right and left without ceasing." At noon on the eighteenth, as Sarrail departed for Beirut, he ordered warplanes and heavy caliber cannon to bombard the city day and night.

The *Manchester Guardian* correspondent interviewed a traveler from Damascus who "describes days and nights of unforgettable terror." The shelling destroyed the famous Souq Hamadiyeh bazaar, the biblical "Street Called Straight," the magnificent Azem Palace and the districts of Shaghur and Meidan. French troops executed insurgents and those who protected them. The *Times* reported that French troops, having murdered two dozen young men in villages southeast of Damascus, brought their corpses to Marjeh Square near the city center. The paper's correspondent wrote:

> Instead of merely exposing the bodies for a space on the spot as an example to other malefactors, in accordance with Eastern custom, and then handing them over to their relatives for decent burial, the French authorities brought them to Damascus. There they attached them to camels and paraded them

through the streets. The ghastly spectacle presented
by the swaying corpses naturally infuriated the excit-
able Damascenes, as indeed the news of the official
adoption of such deterrents will inevitably arouse the
natural indignation of many Frenchmen.

The *Times* reported that the rebels then killed 12
Circassians serving with the French and left their
bodies outside the city's Eastern Gate. "This was the
reply, typical of the spirit of those whom it was intended to humiliate," *The Times* correspondent in Damascus wrote. Forty-eight hours of steady bombardment,
as in Hama, saw the city's leaders begging the rebels
to leave. The *Manchester Guardian* wrote, "The rebels
remained in Damascus until October 20, and only
retired because their presence was given as the cause
of the bombardment."

By the time Sultan al-Atrash's forces arrived,
Damascus was lost. He and his allies, however, took
control of nearby villages and orchards in the fertile
Ghoutha, isolating the capital from the rest of Syria.
Animosity between Damascene civilians and rebels
grew. *The Times* reported that one Druze leader

threatened "the residents of the Meidan quarter that as they had betrayed the Druses on Sunday by refusing to fight they would be the first to suffer from the next attack, which would be made very soon." The French also antagonized the population, devastating villages, machine gunning unarmed civilians and looting houses.

As France gained ground, a Maronite Christian supporter of the rebellion accused them of a crime against humanity. He wrote, "The French army has employed poison gas against the Druze, which affirms French will to exterminate an entire people." No inspectors, as at the end of summer 2013 in Damascus, came to investigate the charge. But pressure on France grew to end the war or to abandon its Mandate.

As with the rebellion against Assad, rival leaderships emerged inside and outside Syria. Fighters, then as now, ignored the external leaders, but they attempted operational coordination under Ramadan Pasha Shallash. Shallash, a bedouin prince, had served as an officer in both the Ottoman and Feisal's armies. Genuine rebel unity, however, proved as elusive as it remains today.

Stephen Henry Longrigg described the rebel leadership in terms that could apply to the present uprising:

> No statesman with a truly national appeal, no con-
> siderable military leader appeared, no central orga-
> nization controlled events, little correlation of effort
> or timing was visible. The Government of Syria
> [Syrians appointed by the French]—ministers,
> officials, departments—gave no countenance
> to the rebellion, those of Great Lebanon and the
> 'Alawis still less; and the greatest part of the public
> abstained, if it could, from overt help to a movement
> which damaged and alarmed it.

French military setbacks were causing severe reper-
cussions at home. Pierre La Mazière, a senator of the
Democratic Left, wrote in *Partant pour la Syrie* that
"we have lost so much money, so many lives, so much
prestige that—Ah, if only we could get out of Syria
without any of the rest of the world noticing it!" Much
of the world demanded that the League of Nations
end the French Mandate. To hang on, the French
government changed leadership in Syria. Général

Maurice Gamelin replaced Général Michaud. A disgraced Sarrail was recalled to Paris, and Senator Henry de Jouvenel became the Mandate's first civilian High Commissioner. He immediately put out feelers to Sultan al-Atrash, paid subsidies to village elders to support the French, offered amnesties to rebels who gave up their arms and traveled to Ankara to bargain with Mustapha Kemal Pasha, the future Atatürk. In exchange for a small parcel of Syrian territory, Turkey cut the arms flow to the rebels.

Disputes among rival rebel leaders crippled their movement, and foreign backers pulled them in different directions. Rebel chiefs deposed and arrested their military commander, Ramadan Shallash. He escaped, surrendered to the French and helped to suppress the rebellion he had led. France escalated its military campaign with aerial bombardment in and around Aleppo and a ground campaign under newly promoted Général Andréa that routed Druze and Sunni forces in the Hauran by the late spring of 1926. Andréa later wrote, "The French flag flew over Suwaida, but there wasn't a single inhabitant left in the town." As with the Americans in Vietnam, destroying villages counted as saving them.

In 1927, Sultan Pasha al-Atrash took refuge in Transjordan and then with Ibn Saud in what would eventually be the Kingdom of Saudi Arabia. The Druze warrior was permitted home 10 years later, and he lived peacefully until 1947, when he launched another doomed revolt against Syria's newly independent government. In the current rebellion, the Druze have remained neutral.

The parallels between then and now are as instructive as the differences, which are many. In the 1920s, fighting did not spread across the region like the current war. While there were Wahhabis from Arabia, there was no equivalent to the Islamic State in Iraq and Syria (ISIS). The French, like the Assads today, held on. The French finally left, as I suspect the Assads will, but that took France another 20 years.

◆

It took less than a year for the armed militias that coalesced into the Free Syrian Army (FSA) and the Islamic Front to displace the pro-democracy demonstrators of 2011. The FSA predicated the success of its rebellion on a repetition of the western air campaign that deposed Muammar Qaddafi in Libya. "When that failed to materialize," Patrick Cockburn wrote in his enlightening *The Jihadis Return: ISIS and the New Sunni Uprising*, "they had no plan B." Without the air support they demanded, the FSA–Islamic Front offensive ground to a stalemate. ISIS came along to supersede the FSA, as the FSA had replaced the protesters. ISIS was more combative, more ruthless, better financed and more effective, using mobility across the desert in Syria and Iraq to launch surprise attacks. It used suicide teams in bomb-laden trucks to open the way into regime strongholds that its rebel adversaries had merely besieged. Moreover, it has achieved the one objective that eluded the FSA: it brought American airpower into the war, but not in the way the FSA wanted. Instead, the Syria war has produced an opposition to Assad so repellent and so antagonistic to western allies in the region that when the air intervention came, it arrived in the guise of the regime's ally in all but name.

The unwillingness of both the regime and the armed opposition to compromise has plunged the

country ever deeper into war. The increasingly
militarized and sectarian character of the opposition,
meanwhile, has pushed both sides toward the killing
of unarmed civilians—effectively, the Lebanization of
the conflict. When I visited Syria in September 2014,
a young woman in Damascus produced a smartphone
from her handbag and asked, "May I show you something?" The phone's screen displayed a sequence of
images. The first was a family photograph of a sparsely
bearded young man in his 20s. Beside him were two
boys, who appeared to be five and six, in T-shirts. The
young man and his sons were smiling. Pointing at the
father, the woman said, "This is my cousin." The next
picture, unlike the first, came from the Internet. It was
the same young man, but his head was severed. Beside
him lay five other men in their 20s whose bloody heads
were similarly stacked on their chests. I looked away.

Her finger skimmed the screen, revealing another
photo of her cousin that she insisted I see. His once
happy face had been impaled on a metal spike. The
spike was one of many in a fence enclosing a public
park in Raqqa, a remote provincial capital on the
Euphrates River in central Syria. Along the fence were

other decapitated heads that children had to pass on their way to the playground. The woman's cousin and his five comrades were soldiers in the Syrian army's 17th Reserve Division. ISIS had captured them when it overran the Tabqa military airfield, about 25 miles from ISIS headquarters in Raqqa, on August 24. The family's sole hope was that the young man was already dead when they cut off his head. There was no question of returning the body or holding a funeral. The woman explained that her cousin had recently turned down a chance to leave his unit for a safer post near his home. It would not be right, he reasoned, for him, as a member of Syrian President Assad's minority Alawite sect, to desert his fellow soldiers who were Sunni. He stayed with them, and he died with them.

The first victims of a war in Syria were always going to be the religious minorities. The Alawites and the Christians, who each make up about 10 percent of the population, have found security under the Assad regime. The Alawites—whose doctrines are related to those of Shia Islam, and whose rule is opposed on principle by many Sunnis—are concentrated in the west near the Mediterranean. The Syrian government does not publish casualty figures by sect, but martyrs' notices pasted on the walls in Jabal Alawia, the Alawite heartland in the hills east of the port of Latakia, indicate that the Alawites have suffered a disproportionate share of deaths in the war to preserve the Alawite president. A myth promulgated by the Sunni Islamist opposition is that the Alawites have been the main beneficiaries of 44 years of Assad family rule over Syria, but evidence of Alawite wealth outside the presidential clan and entourage is hard to find. The meager peasant landholdings that marked the pre-Assad era are still the rule in Jabal Alawia, where most families live on the fruits of a few acres. Some Alawite merchants have done better in the seaside cities of Latakia and Tartous, but so have Sunni, Druze and Christian businessmen. This may explain in part why, from my own observations, a considerable proportion of Syrian Sunnis, who comprise about 75 percent of the population, have not taken up arms against the regime. If they had, the regime would not have survived.

The Alawite monopoly of the armed forces is, like much of Syria, a legacy of foreign intervention. As Dr. Hafiz Jemalli, the Baath Party founding member, told me in 1987, "When we resisted the French, we had to act as a unified people. Now we are divided. We are Muslim. We are Alawi. We are Druze. We are Christian. How did it happen? Syria in the 1940s was liberated from sectarianism, but now we are divided into sects. The army is now composed of Alawi officers. A majority of our army is a minority of our people. It comes only by chance?"

The rising number of Alawite young men killed or severely wounded while serving in the army and in regime-backed militias has led to resentment among people who have no choice other than to fight for President Assad and to keep their state's institutions intact. Their survival, as long as Sunni jihadists kill them wherever they find them, requires them to support a regime that many of them oppose and blame for forcing them into this predicament. After my friend's cousin and his comrades were decapitated at Tabqa and their corpses left on the streets of Raqqa, ISIS publicly executed another 200 captured soldiers. It was then that someone, said to be an Alawite dissident, declared on Facebook, "Assad is in his palace and our sons are in their graves."

Alawite frustration is matched by that of the now-marginalized nonviolent opponents of Assad's rule. But like the Alawites who grumble off the record, they are powerless. As difficult as the Alawites' position now is, their geographic concentration at least means they have a territorial base from which to negotiate their survival no matter who takes power. (In Beirut, just before I crossed the border to Syria, Walid Jumblatt, Lebanon's Druze leader, told me he had advised his fellow Druze in Syria to join the rebellion. "They swim in a Sunni sea, not an Alawite sea," he said. He referred to the Algerians, the Harkis, who sided with the French during the war of independence: some were killed, and the remainder found refuge in France.) The Christians, by contrast, are thinly dispersed among Aleppo, Damascus, Wadi Nasara, Qamishli and other parts of the country. Shia-Sunni fighting in Iraq after 2003 had precipitated the flight of nearly two million Iraqi Christians to Syria; there was always a risk of a similar exodus from Syria should the anti-regime rebellion descend into a tribal and sectarian war. Where are they and Syria's indigenous Christians supposed to find refuge? Do the West's holy warriors want them to leave and for Syria to be as purely Sunni as their favorite Mideast statelet, Saudi Arabia?

Many Christians view the opposition's driving force as Sunni fundamentalism battling a powerful Alawite minority. The fundamentalists would deprive them, as well as secular Sunnis, of social freedoms. Gregory III Laham, the Melkite Catholic Patriarch of Antioch, warned early in the rebellion against the "criminals and even fundamentalist Muslims who cry for *jihad*. This is why we fear that giving way to violence will only lead to chaos." An Armenian high school teacher, whom I have known for many years, became uncharacteristically loquacious when explaining her support for the Assad regime. She told me in Aleppo in 2012, barely a year into the rebellion:

I'm free. I am safe.... "You're a *kafir* [unbeliever]": I have not heard that phrase for 30 years. At the school, some of my friends are Muslim Brothers. They respect me, and I respect them. Who is responsible for that?...Look at this terror. Is this what Obama wants? Is this what Sarkozy wants? Let them leave us alone. If we don't like our president, we won't

elect him. From a woman who is 60 years old, and
I've been free for 30 years. I should be afraid to go
out? I should cover myself? Women should live like
donkeys? . . . We are citizens. We are equal.

She, along with many other residents of Aleppo, has
installed a steel-reinforced front door to her house.
Tales of the rape, kidnapping and murder of Christians
in Homs, the city halfway between Aleppo and Damascus that became the bastion of the revolution, created
unease among their coreligionists throughout Syria. At
the same time, cameras have recorded civilian deaths
there from attacks by government forces. In Aleppo,
bombs that damaged buildings occupied by the
security forces took with them nearby Christian apartments, schools and churches. The chaos has already
led to large-scale emigration of the Christian communities who have lived in Syria for two millennia. "Many
Christians have left," Dr. Samir Katerji, a 58-year-old
architect and member of the Syrian Orthodox Church,
told me in mid-2012. "Many Armenians have bought
houses in Armenia. Even the Muslims are leaving."
Katerji, who designed the amphitheater for outdoor

films in the Aleppo Citadel, had "visited my aunt's house," a local euphemism for going to prison, several times. The security services arrested him for his outspoken criticism of the Assad regime and the Baath Party. A year after we spoke, Katerji migrated to the United States. Indeed, many opposition members of minority communities insist that their security is part of the historical nature of Syria rather than the gift of the regime that came to power with Hafez al-Assad's bloodless coup. A Christian woman, who spent several months in prison for unspecified political crimes a few years ago, told me, "It's wrong to say the government was helping the minorities. They are using the minorities."

Fear forces people into the ostensible safety of sectarian or ethnic enclaves, repeating a pattern established during the civil war in Lebanon and the American occupation of Iraq. Mixed neighborhoods, so prominent a feature of Syrian life now and in the past, are making way for segregated ghettos where people feel safe among their own. Nabil al-Samman, an engineering professor in Damascus, wrote ominously in *Syria Today*, "The current crisis proves that you cannot depend on the government, but only on your immediate family, your tribe, and others' charity." Some Christians who fled from Homs following vicious fighting there between the army and the dissident Free Syrian Army blamed Muslim fundamentalists for seizing their houses to use as firing positions, while others left because of the violence or the threat of kidnapping, rape and murder. Alawites loyal to the regime in and around Homs stand accused of killing Sunni men and raping Sunni women, while the rebels are blamed for committing the same crimes against Alawites. The effect has been the same: to drive each out of the other's areas and into tribal *laagers* that further divide the country into armed and hostile camps.

Mufti Hassoun's criticism of the opposition has been stronger than his criticism of the state. He has received death threats. "When I refused to leave Syria," he says, "they threatened me on my cell phone," referring to callers whose numbers were in Saudi Arabia. "They left messages." When he did not answer, his enemies took their revenge. On October 2, 2011, his 22-year-old son, Sariya, was driving with one of his university professors from the countryside to Aleppo when armed men fired on their car and killed them both. The mufti recalled the murder in our conversation, wiping tears from his cheeks: "He was 22 years old, a student at the university. What did he do to be killed? At his funeral, I said I forgive you all. I expected them to show remorse. They said we don't need your forgiveness. We are going to kill you. They say this on television in Saudi Arabia, Egypt and Britain. They say the mufti of Syria speaks of Christianity in a positive way. He believes in dialogue, even with Israelis and non-believers. He goes to churches. They say I do not represent Islam. When you say a mufti does not represent Islam, it's a *fatwa* to kill him. This is the Arab revolution."

While lamenting Syria's lack of basic political freedoms, including free speech and assembly, Samir Katerji acknowledged that "we have social freedom. We are free to declare our thoughts and beliefs and to practice our Christianity." He condemned murderers within the regime, but had no faith in its armed opponents: "Inside the opposition are also murderers who will not allow stability."

One Christian said to me in a whisper, "I shit on this revolution, because it is forcing me into the arms of the regime."

IV.
"THE REVOLUTION
DIED IN ALEPPO"

ARCHAEOLOGISTS BELIEVE THAT HUMAN beings settled on the hilltop that became Aleppo—some 225 miles north of Damascus—around 8,000 years ago. Cuneiform tablets from the third millennium BC record the construction of a temple to a chariot-riding storm god, usually called Hadad. Mid-second-millennium Hittite archives point to the settlement's growing political and economic power. Its Arabic name, Haleb, is said to derive from Haleb Ibrahim, "Milk of Abraham," for the sheep's milk the biblical patriarch offered to travelers in Aleppo's environs. Successive conquerors planted their standards on the ramparts of a fortress that they enlarged and reinforced over centuries to complete the impressive stone Citadel that dominates the city today.

"It is an excellent city without equal for the beauty of its location, the grace of its construction and the size and symmetry of its marketplaces," wrote the great Arab voyager Ibn Batuta when he visited in 1348. During the Renaissance, Aleppo was Islam's third-most important city after Constantinople and Cairo. The modern Lebanese historian Antoine Abdel Nour praised it in his *Introduction à l'histoire urbaine de la Syrie ottomane*:

> Metropolis of a vast region, situated at the crossroads of the Arab, Turkish, and Iranian worlds, it represents without doubt the most beautiful example of the Arab city. Its beauty reveals itself in the elegance of its stone architecture, redolent of historic links to Byzantium and Venice; and in the diversity of its peoples—Arabs, Armenians, Kurds, eleven Christian denominations, Sunni Muslims, a smattering of dissident Shiite sects from Druze to Ismailis, ancient families of urban patricians as well as peasant and Bedouin immigrants from the plains—that makes it a microcosm of all Syria.

A trading entrepôt that once stood on the Silk Road, Aleppo was Syria's workshop and marketplace, and its region generated as much as 65 percent of the national wealth apart from oil. Factories making textiles from Syrian cotton, as well as medicines and furniture, dominated the industrial zones outside the city and provided work to thousands.

Until now, it has stood for just about everything al-Qaeda of Iraq and ISIS oppose. No city in Syria is more mixed or more diverse. "Aleppo (Haleb) is the best built city in the Turkish dominions," reported the English traveler William Eton in his 1789 *A Survey of the Turkish Empire*, "and the people are reputed the most polite." Tolerance has been its hallmark since Ottoman times. Documentary records of Ottoman Turkey's dominion over Aleppo from 1516 to 1918 portray communities of Muslims, Christians and Jews living in the same neighborhoods. Unlike Tunis, where Jews were obliged to rent living space, Aleppo's governors imposed no restrictions on house ownership by members of any religious group or by women. It was not unusual for large mansions to be divided into apartments in which Muslim, Jewish and Christian families dwelled with little more than the usual rancor that afflicts neighbors everywhere. Unlike more xenophobic Damascus, Aleppo encouraged European merchants to trade and live within the city walls. The European powers, beginning with Venice in the 16th century, established in Aleppo the first consulates in the Ottoman Empire to guard the interests of their expatriate subjects. Reputed descendants of Marco Polo, the Marcopoli family, retained the office of Italian honorary consul well into the 20th century.

In a neglected corner of the old Bahsita Quarter, behind several old office buildings, stands a monument to Aleppo's historic mélange. The Bandara Synagogue was built on a site of Jewish worship that predates by two centuries the 637 AD Arab-Muslim conquest of Aleppo. Its courtyard of fine cut-stone arches and domes resembles the arcaded cloister of the nearby al-Qadi Mosque. The Jewish community of Aleppo, like its larger counterpart in Damascus, gradually made its way to New York after the founding of Israel. When the last Jews departed *en masse* in 1992, after then President Hafez al-Assad lifted restrictions on their emigration, Damascus and Aleppo were suddenly bereft of an ancient and significant strand of their social fabrics. The synagogue, restored by Syrian Jewish exiles, is the forlorn relic of a community that thrived for ages before vanishing under the weight of war between Syria and Israel. It is also a harbinger of what Aleppo's Christians see as their fate if the latest uprising leads to domination by Sunni Muslim fundamentalists.

The regimes of Hafez al-Assad since 1970 and his son Bashar since 2000 left Aleppo's gracious city center with little to rebel against, even if the rural poor—driven into the suburbs by drought, unemployment and ambition—had legitimate complaints that went unnoticed in the lavish villas along the River Qoweik. Many of Aleppo's inhabitants were old enough to remember the last time the city was the scene of a rebellion, in 1979. Its outcome gave them little hope that a repetition would be anything other than disaster. Yet with the revolt in the countryside creeping closer on all sides, the ancient city had no more chance of remaining aloof than a log cabin in the midst of a forest fire.

In normal times, the best way to travel the 200 miles from Damascus to Aleppo was by road, with a lunch break in the gardens beside Hama's Roman aqueducts. When the rebellion expanded in May 2011 from Dera'a in the south to Homs, cutting the

Damascus–Aleppo highway, flying became a safer option. Still, for the first year of the uprising, Aleppins thought they could stay out of the conflict. As late as February 2012, on one of my visits, the city's mercantile elite had yet to leave and their businesses were still functioning. Aleppo's famed olive oil was plentiful in the labyrinthine *souqs* of vaulted stone near the Citadel. Most people shared relief bordering on complacency that their city had avoided the violence engulfing the rest of the country. Aleppo's cosmopolitanism, they seemed to feel, made it different. The only pogrom against its Christian minority had taken place in 1851, when the number of dead was small, and the crime was never repeated. The city's relative prosperity kept much of the population satisfied, despite the suppression of political opinion.

On my return six months later, Aleppo's airport was nearly deserted. Taxis no longer risked the trip from town without the guarantee of a fare, so I had arranged for friends to send a driver they trusted. He grabbed my bag and ran to his car, turned the key in the ignition and made a hasty sign of the cross. Then he broke into a sweat. About a quarter mile from the airport, an abrupt

U-turn took us off the highway to a deserted access road. The few buildings here had been hit by high-velocity ordnance and all of them, except a warehouse that Syrian government troops were using as a command post beside sandbags and a limp flag, were gutted and empty. About a mile on, a truck-mounted antiaircraft gun on a bank above the road loomed into view. The driver turned back onto the desolate highway. Suddenly, burned tires, cement blocks and debris blocked the road and forced us into what would have been oncoming traffic, had there been any. Gas stations were wrecked, and gasoline trucks lay charred beside the road. Rough cinder block houses for the poor stood on either side of us, pocked by artillery. A few miles farther, as we entered the city proper, the driver relaxed at the sight of pedestrians and a few cars. Near a traffic roundabout, people at a makeshift street market were hawking bright red and green tomatoes, huge potatoes, eggplants, zucchini, apples and pomegranates. The driver pointed at the carts, which had not been there in April, and said, "They wanted freedom. Here's their freedom!"

The city had acquired internal borders. On my first night back, a friend walked with me to the edge of the safe Sulaimaniya neighborhood. Where once we would have walked easily from Sulaimaniya into adjoining Jdaideh without noticing any difference, Jdaideh had become another world. Cars had been parked to block the entrances to its streets, and none of its lights were on. Sulaimaniya's street lamps shone on modern cafés filled with men and women enjoying coffee, sweets or *narguiles*. Jdaideh, only 50 yards away, had been depopulated since the rebels entered it a month earlier. Wherever the rebels went, the army attacked them and residents fled.

I wanted to visit the *souqs* in the morning, but my friend told me that continued fighting there made it impossible. Who burned the *souqs* a few weeks earlier? "That was the Free Syrian Army," my friend said. "We are caught between two bad powers. As you know, I don't like the dictatorship. But these people are showing themselves as worse."

Aleppins who grew up with regime repression have discovered the anarchic brutality of life in "liberated" zones. *Guardian* correspondent Ghaith Abdul Ahad attended a meeting of 32 senior rebel commanders in the city in late 2012. A former regime colonel, who had assumed command of Aleppo's military council, told his comrades: "Even the people are fed up with us. We were liberators, but now they denounce us and demonstrate against us." Abdul Ahad described the rebel looting of a school:

> The men ferried some of the tables, sofas and chairs outside the school and piled them up at the street corner. Computers and monitors followed.

> A fighter registered the loot in a big notebook. "We are keeping it safe in a warehouse," he said.

> Later in the week, I saw the school's sofas and computers sitting comfortably in the commander's new apartment.

> Another fighter, a warlord named Abu Ali who controls a few square blocks of Aleppo as his personal fief, said: "They blame us for the destruction. Maybe they are right, but had the people of Aleppo supported the revolution from the beginning, this wouldn't have happened."

Another friend said of the rebels who had come to dominate large swathes of his city: "They entered Aleppo. Aleppo didn't enter the conflict." He is a businessman, previously happy to be quoted but now insisting I not print his name. Members of his family have been kidnapped, and he has paid large sums at the end of tortuous negotiations for their release. Where Aleppins once feared the state's many *mukhabarat* (intelligence agencies), they had now become wary of additional retribution from the *Jaish al-Hurr*, the Free Army, and its associated militias. Another friend said, "The opposition thought Aleppo would welcome them. It didn't, except in the outskirts, where the very poor and the rural people came in." While espousing the revolution, some in the poorer districts nonetheless sought to exclude the rebels from their neighborhoods. In one of the poorest, Bani Zayd, where many people sift through the city's garbage to make a living, the area's elders delivered a letter to the Free Army:

> We cheered the Free Army. But what is happening today is a crime against the inhabitants of

our neighborhood. For there are no offices for government security or the *shabihah* [pro-regime Alawite gangs]. However, the groups that have taken position in the neighborhood cannot defend it. ... We, the elders of Bani Zayd neighborhood, are responsible for making this statement and demand that battalions of the Free Army which have entered the neighborhood leave it and join battles on hot fronts. ... This would ensure the return of calm to the neighborhood and would end the random shelling [by regime forces] of a poor neighborhood housing thousands of displaced people.

Bani Zayd's residents were natural supporters of the revolution, but their commitment did not extend to tactics that left them vulnerable to retaliation by the regime. The Free Army's inability to defend most of the areas it occupied soon turned other potential supporters against it. What is the point, they asked, of inviting the regime to bombard an area that cannot be held? There was particular resentment in Aleppo of the rebel occupation of the *souqs* in late September 2012. Before that, they were much as a former Australian ambassador to Syria, Ross Burns, described them in his definitive study of Syrian antiquities, *Monuments of Syria: An Historical Guide*:

> Largely unchanged since the 16th century (some go back as far as the 13th), [the *souqs*] preserve superbly the atmosphere of the Arab/Turkish mercantile tradition. In summer, the vaulted roofs provide cool refuge; in winter, protection from the rain and cold. While many of the products on sale have been updated, there are still areas where the rope-maker, tent outfitter and sweetmeat seller ply their trade much as they have done for centuries.

The majestic lanes of markets and ateliers were the city's commercial hub, but also the embodiment of its spirit. Although the rebels accused the regime of starting the fires, most people, even the rebels' supporters, blamed the rebels. The Free Army followed its assault on the *souqs* with one 500-kilogram and two 1000-kilogram bombs in cars near an officers' club and the main post office in Saadallah Jabri Square, the city's central park, on the morning of October 3.

A Syrian journalist who witnessed the explosions that killed more than 40 people and left another 125 injured told me, "There are divisions within the Free Army. If it had a few hundred people, they could have occupied city hall and proclaimed Aleppo a liberated city." That they didn't was as much a measure of rebel disunity as of tactics that strike blows here and there without capitalizing on them.

At the beginning of 2015, Aleppo was the major zone of contention between the regime and the rival opposition forces, who fight one another as much as they do the army. The road north to Aleppo from Homs remained precarious, until rebels surrendered their positions in Homs and departed with their light weapons under United Nations supervision. A Human Rights Watch report identified hundreds of sites in Aleppo that had been attacked, often with barrel bombs, by government forces. The battle for Aleppo is a war for Syria itself. In both political and military terms, Syria's commercial capital is vital to both sides. Yet both the regime and its armed opponents are alienating the people they are ostensibly trying to cultivate, as they jointly demolish Aleppo's economy, the historic monuments that give the city its unique charm and identity, the lives and safety of its citizens and the social cohesion that had made it a model of intersectarian harmony. Another friend confided, "The revolution died in Aleppo. They [the rebels] thought they would win the battle of Aleppo. They thought the people of Aleppo would support them."

Syria's war is anything its fighters want it to be. It is a class war of the suburban proletariat against a state army financed by the bourgeoisie. It is a sectarian war in which the Sunni Arab majority is fighting to displace an Alawi ruling class. It is a holy war of Sunni Muslims against all manifestations of Shiism, especially the Alawite variety. The social understandings on which Aleppo prided itself are unraveling. Muslim fundamentalists have targeted Christian churches and Shiite mosques. Arabs have fought Kurds. Iraqi Shiites and Sunnis have crossed the border to fight each other in Syria.

In early 2012, Aleppin Christians were for the most part in favor of the regime or neutral, hoping to avoid the attentions of either side. When I met the Syrian Orthodox metropolitan of Aleppo, Mar Gregorios Yohanna Ibrahim, that Easter, he said with an encouraging laugh, "Am I worried? Yes. Am

I afraid? No." Aleppo was quiet, though conflicts in the rest of Syria were clear harbingers of the earthquake about to hit. At the time, Mar Gregorios was convinced that the regime and the opposition could resolve their differences: "If we solve our internal problem and sit down and talk, we can have a constructive dialogue. We can gradually rebuild our society." As bishop of a small community of about 200,000 in Syria, he avoided committing himself to either side while accepting that the regime had protected Christians.

By the end of the year, his worry had turned to fear. On the night I saw him in the sheltered confines of his rectory in the middle of Aleppo, he had just received a shock. "I was optimistic for the last weeks, but I visited my school today. Out of 550 students, only 50 are left." Along with his discovery that every day about 20 of his local congregation were receiving visas for foreign countries, the collapse of the school had changed him from the jocular, relaxed prelate I met in October to a profoundly shaken man with little hope for his country's future. "The issue now," he said, "is how to convince the president to step down." This was the first time I had heard a Christian bishop call for Bashar al-Assad to end the war by leaving office.

Like Vichy France, Syria is divided into regime supporters, *résistants* and *attentistes* who await the outcome before choosing sides. Most of those I spoke to in all three camps rejected military intervention by the US, Britain, France and, especially, Turkey to solve their problems. The Armenian Catholic Archbishop Boutros Maryati recalled that many Armenians in Aleppo came from the massacres in Turkey and were forced to leave their country in 1915. "They found in Aleppo a secure shelter, have the rights of any Syrian and became part of the Syrian identity. They had many martyrs who defended Syria. Psychologically and spiritually, we have some worries—especially intervention by Turkey. We are afraid to be forced into a new emigration."

Even the non-Armenian bishops who spoke to me in Aleppo and Damascus dreaded invasion by the Turkish army. Turkey, they pointed out, does not allow churches to conduct services freely as Syria does, and it prevented Arabs in Hatay province, part of Syria until the French gave it to Turkey in 1938, from speaking their own language. In Syria, they can speak whatever language they want. In Aleppo, Muslim children make up the majority in most Christian-run schools where much of the teaching is in French. As the Armenians fear the Turks, Alawites and Christians fear Sunni Salafists who chant:

> *Massihiyeh ala Beirut,*
> *Alawiyeh ala Taboot.*
> Christians to Beirut,
> Alawis to the coffin.

One of the few activists who gave permission for me to quote him by name was Zaidoun al-Zoabi, professor at the Arab European University in Damascus. He was dismissed from his job for political reasons in February 2011. He lamented, "Aleppo has been destroyed . . . The country is being destroyed." Zoabi has struggled to keep alive the original, peaceful revolution that began in March 2011 and was superseded by the armed rebellion. (Regime security forces arrested Zoabi after our meeting. On his release from nearly a month in prison, he left the country.) A young Syrian businessman whose family has long been at odds with the regime blamed the armed opposition for trying to bring down the regime by force: "You cannot just break a regime like this; it is built to last. The regime is built for this." The regime, which in its early days immunized itself against coups d'état with the arrest of suspected dissidents in the army and constant surveillance, made itself rebellion-proof in the wake of the 1979 uprising in Aleppo.

The 1979 revolt provides an instructive comparison with the present rebellion. A US Defense Intelligence Agency (DIA) report of May 1982, "Syria: Muslim Brotherhood Pressure Intensifies," analyzed that insurrection and Assad's response: "In early 1979, encouraged by the Islamic Revolution in Iran, the Syrian Muslim Brotherhood developed a plan to trigger a similar popular revolution in Syria to oust Assad." The Brotherhood's first salvo was a massacre of 83 Alawite cadets on June 16 at the artillery school in Aleppo. That led to widespread arrests and gunfights in Aleppo's streets. By the following June, in the opinion of the DIA, "President Assad had broken the back of the Muslim Brotherhood challenge."

The Muslim Brothers who escaped evolved a two-pronged plan for insurgency and a coup against Assad by their sympathizers in the army. The DIA report stated:

> In early 1982, however, Syrian security uncovered the coup plot and began to intensify their operations against dissidents within the country. As a result, the Muslim Brotherhood felt pressured into initiating the uprising in Hama which began on 2 February 1982.

The Brotherhood hoped Aleppo, Homs and other large cities would imitate Hama and initiate a new era. The other cities did not rise, and the Defense Brigades of Hafez's ruthless brother Rifaat annihilated the Brothers in Hama. The DIA put the number of probable casualties at 2,000, although later Amnesty International concluded that as many as 25,000 people died.

For the Iranian Revolution of 1979, read the Arab Spring of 2010 and 2011. If Syria was not Iran, it isn't Tunisia or Egypt either. The new rebellion has pitted Sunni against Alawi and other minorities, but more importantly it seethes with the class resentments that the displaced rural poor acquired when they confronted urban luxury. Droughts between 2007 and 2011 exacerbated the hardships of country life, driving many people into Aleppo.

This was not new. In 1987, I spent time among the peasants along the Euphrates east of Aleppo. Their village, called Yusuf Basha, was earmarked for evacuation under a scheme to build a hydroelectric dam. I returned to Aleppo from the east and saw peasants drying wheat on the sidewalks as they did in their villages. I wrote:

Before, I had seen the city of Aleppo growing along the hilltops, as the suburbs ate into the countryside. Now, I realized that the village had come to the city, planting itself outside and growing in. The poor farmers were bringing their customs, their ways, to cosmopolitan Aleppo, as they were to Damascus and Beirut. They were turning their apartments into compact versions of their mud houses—the families sleeping together in one room, cooking in another, washing in another, each room like one of the little huts around their yards. It was not poverty,

but tradition, that put a whole family into one room.
This was the only security they had in a city that was
at once unwelcoming and alien.

That return to Aleppo was an enlightening moment,
when I saw the city as new arrivals from the village did.
If Aleppo had accommodated them, slowly absorbing
them into the city's economic and cultural life, as it had
in centuries past, they might not have welcomed rebels
from backgrounds similar to theirs. The neoliberal
economic policies that Bashar al-Assad introduced
when he succeeded his father in 2000 exacerbated
their plight. The beneficiaries were newly privatized
bankers, Bashar's cousins who obtained licenses to
sell mobile phones, middlemen and brokers with
urban educations and customs, not the newly landless
trying without money or education to adapt to metropolitan life. For them to react as they are now doing is
part of an ancient pattern that I noticed on that return
to Aleppo 25 years ago:

For the first time in all my years in the Levant, I saw
how corrupting the peasant and the bedouin found

the city. Arab tradition said that every other generation brought a wave of reformers, religious zealots,
from the desert to purify the city. It had happened in
Saudi Arabia many times, lasting until the luxury of
city life corrupted that generation's sons. I wondered
whether it would happen in Syria.

Some 25 years later, it is happening. The human cost is
unimaginable, and growing.

V.
THE DEADLANDS

FOLK MEMORIES ENDURE, MOTHERS' AND grandmothers' sagas trumping documents in neglected archives. What will Syria's youth, when they are old, tell their children? All will have stories of cowering in their flimsy houses while bombs fell, of the deadening existence of refugee camps, or of escapes through treacherous seas and perilous highways to uncertain lives in strange lands. My maternal grandmother left Mount Lebanon, then part of Syria, as a child in the late nineteenth century during a confrontation between the Christians of her village and their Ottoman rulers. Although her father was killed a few months before she was born, she told me many times how he faced Turkish troops on horseback as if she had witnessed it. I don't know what really happened; but her stories, including of a river so cold it could crack a watermelon in two, remain undeniable truths to her descendants.

Syrians today are enduring a brutal, unending ordeal that reenacts the drama of their ancestors during a prior war exactly one century ago that their families, novelists, and poets preserved for them. What we know as World War I was to Syrians *Seferberlik,* from the Arabic for "travel across the land," when military conscription, forced labor battalions, machine-age weaponry, arbitrary punishment, pestilence, and famine undid in four years all that the Ottomans had achieved over the previous four centuries. The Palestinian sociologist Salim Tamari saw that period as

> four miserable years of tyranny symbolized by the military dictatorship of Ahmad Cemal [or Jemal] Pasha in Syria, *seferberlik* (forced conscription and exile), and the collective hanging of Arab patriots in Beirut's Burj Square on August 15, 1916.

Turkey's institutionalized sadism added to the woes of Syrians, who grew hungrier each year because of the Anglo-French blockade that kept out, as American and

European Union sanctions do today, many of the basic staples needed for survival.

No part of what was then called Syria, which included today's Lebanon, Jordan, and Israel, avoided the cataclysm. An economics professor at Beirut's Syrian Protestant College wrote, "You never saw a starving person, did you? May the Almighty preserve you from this sight!!!" Rafael de Nogales, a freebooting Venezuelan officer in the Ottoman army, recorded that

> Aleppo kept on filling up with mendicant and pest-stricken deportees who died in the streets by the hundreds, and infected the rest of the population to such an extent that on some days the funeral carts were insufficient to carry the dead to the cemeteries.

The locust infestation of 1915 and hoarding by Beirut's grain merchants aggravated a famine so severe that there were many tales of cannibalism. Hana Mina, a Syrian novelist born just after the war, wrote in his novel *Fragments of Memory*, "During the *Safar Barrlik*, mothers . . . became like cats and ate their children." A half-million out of four million inhabitants in

Greater Syria perished from starvation, disease, and violence.

The four and a half years since March 2011 are recreating the suffering of a century ago: malnutrition, starvation, epidemics, the exodus of most of the population to other parts of Syria or to foreign lands, the brutality of the combatants, the traumatization of children, and Great Power preference for victory over the inhabitants' well-being. An anonymous Syrian poet, in words his twenty-first-century countrymen might echo, wrote:

> The Drums of War are beating their sad rhythm
> And the living people, wrapped in their shroud
> Believing the war will not last a year . . .
> Dear God, may this fifth year be the end of it.

That fifth year, 1918, was the end of it, but this century's war is heading toward its sixth year with no prospect of a conclusion. Thousands of Russian military advisers are joining the fight on behalf of President Bashar al-Assad, as Iran and its Lebanese surrogate, Hezbollah, have from the beginning. The United States and its regional allies are increasing the flow of arms to the rebels. What was true in 2011 holds today: neither side has the power to defeat the other.

Returning to Damascus last month after a year's absence, I discovered new dynamics. Last year, the regime seemed to be gaining the upper hand. The rebels had evacuated Homs, the first city they conquered. Jihadists had withdrawn from the Armenian village of Kessab near the Turkish border in the northwest, and Assad's army was encroaching into the rebel-held Damascus suburbs. The rise of the self-proclaimed Islamic State (ISIS) was causing the foreign supporters of the rebellion to recalibrate and consider making Assad an ally against the fanatics who threatened to export the war to the West itself. Popular complaints focused on electricity shortages, loss of wages, the hazards of sporadic rebel shelling, and the hardships of daily survival.

A year later, all has changed. The regime is in retreat. It lost Idlib province in the north. Jihadi forces backed by Turkey have surrounded the vital commercial entrepôt and cosmopolitan center of Aleppo. The jewel of the desert, the ancient Roman and Arab city of Palmyra, is in the hands of ISIS militants who tortured and beheaded an eighty-two-year-old antiquities scholar and are destroying one ancient monument after another. Young men are emigrating to avoid being drafted to fight for any side in what seems like an eternal war.

The few who remain are sons without brothers, who cannot be conscripted under Syrian law, which recognizes that the loss of an only son means the end of the family. As in World War I, this has led to a surfeit of women supporting their families by any means necessary. Inflation is around 40 percent. Estimates of territory held by regime opponents run from the United Nations' 65 percent to the *Jane's* report of 83 percent, while the UN estimates that anywhere between 60 and 80 percent of the population still within the country now live in areas held by the government. Migration from rebel-held areas into the capital has, as measured by the company that collects city waste, multiplied Damascus's population five times, from about two million before the war to ten million today. Elizabeth Hoff, Director of the World Health Organization in Syria, said, "Nine out of ten people in Damascus hospitals are not from Damascus. They come from Raqqa and elsewhere." Raqqa is now held by ISIS.

Supporters of the original uprising of 2011 imagined a quick victory over the dictator along the lines of what happened in Tunisia, Egypt, and Libya. A Syrian friend of mine, now living in exile, told me the American ambassador, Robert Ford, just before he withdrew from Damascus in October 2011, tried to recruit him to take part in a government that he promised would shortly replace Assad's. When the French ambassador to Syria, Eric Chevallier, left Damascus on March 6, 2012, barely one year into the war, he told friends that he would be back when a post-Assad government was installed "in two months."

Since then, with Assad still in power, the death toll has climbed to at least 320,000. Out of a total population of 22 million before the war, more than 4 million Syrians have fled the country, and another 7.6 million are displaced within it. With Syria's neighbors overwhelmed, hundreds of thousands of Syrians are now trying to seek refuge in Europe, causing one of the greatest challenges to the EU in its history. The government-in-waiting that Ford and other Western diplomats had hoped to install in Damascus has collapsed amid internal squabbling and a lack of committed fighters.

The only forces fighting with success against the Assad regime are Sunni Muslim holy warriors who are destroying all that was best in Syria: its mosaic of different sects and ethnic communities—including Christians, Druze, Turkmen, Yazidis, and Kurds, along with Alawites and Sunni Arabs—its heritage of ancient monuments, its ancient manuscripts and Sumerian tablets, its industrial and social infrastructure, and its tolerance of different social customs. "The worst thing is not the violence," the Armenian Orthodox primate of Syria, Bishop Armash Nalbandian, told me. "It is this new hatred."

In a war that is now in its fifth year and has left little of pre-war Syrian society intact, everyone seems to be asking, in one way or another, how did we get here and where are we going? What is the reason for the savagery from all sides in what has become an apocalyptic struggle for dominance and survival? Why, back in 2011, did the regime shoot at demonstrators who were not shooting at the government, and why did the uprising come to depend on a contest of weapons, in which the regime would hold the upper hand?

The United States encouraged the opposition from the beginning. The *Guardian* reported on October 24, 2011:

The US vice-president, Joe Biden, last week triggered
speculation by saying that the military model used in
Libya—US air power in support of rebels on the ground
backed by French and British special forces—could be
used elsewhere.

It did not happen, although the CIA trained rebels in
Jordan and Turkey, Saudi Arabia and Qatar provided
arms, and Turkey opened its borders to jihadis from
around the world to wreak havoc in Syria. However,
Western predictions of the regime's quick demise were
soon shown to be false.

A consensus among the US, Britain, France, Saudi
Arabia, Qatar, Turkey, and Israel held that Assad's strategic alliance with Iran was detrimental to all of their
interests. These powers perceived an expansionist Iran
using to its advantage indigenous Shiites in Bahrain,
Yemen, and Lebanon along with the Alawite minority in
Syria, which has long been allied with the Shiites. They
sought to eclipse the "Shiite Crescent" on the battlefields
of Syria. Rather than eliminate Iranian influence in Syria,
however, they have multiplied it. The Syrian military,
once an independent secular force that looked to Iran

and Hezbollah for men and weapons, now relies on Iran to determine strategy in a war of survival that, if the regime wins, will leave the Iranians in a stronger position than they were before the war.

Major military decisions come from the Iranian General Qassem Soleimani, the astute commander of the Iranian Revolutionary Guards' elite Quds force, rather than from Syria's discredited officer class. In Aleppo, residents speak of an Iranian officer called Jawal commanding Shiite militia forces from Iran, Iraq, Afghanistan, and Lebanon against the Sunni jihadists who have the city almost surrounded.

"Most people feel we are under Iranian occupation," a Sunni businessman tells me, expressing a widespread perception in government-held areas. A Sunni shopkeeper in Damascus's old city pointed to some bearded militiamen at a checkpoint near his front door and complained that Shiites from outside Syria were taking over his neighborhood. This disquiet is not restricted to the Sunnis. "I'm thinking of leaving," a friend in Damascus told me. "I'm Alawite, and I'm secular, but I don't like this Islamicization that came with Hezbollah."

The growth of Iranian influence on the Syrian government pits two theocratic ideologies, the late Ayatollah Khomeini's *wali al faqih,* or "rule of (Islamic) jurists," versus the Saudi-inspired Wahhabi fundamentalism of ISIS as well as the Turkish-backed, al-Qaeda-affiliated Jabhat al-Nusra. This has led many Syrians who don't subscribe to Sunni or Shiite fundamentalist ideology to welcome Russian military engagement. In recent weeks, Russia has pledged to continue military support for Assad's forces. Many Syrians welcome this less to confront ISIS and its like-minded jihadi rivals than to offset the Iranians and their clients from Hezbollah, the Iraqi militias, and Afghanistan's Shiite Hazaras.

The West and its local allies are suffering the unintended consequences of their policies, as the Ottomans did when they declared war on the Allies in 1914. Turkey's goals then were to take Egypt back from the British and expand its empire into the Turkish-speaking Muslim lands of the Russian Empire. To say that the Young Turk triumvirate guiding Sultan Mehmed V's policies miscalculated is a historic understatement: rather than achieve either objective, they lost all of their empire outside Anatolia, disgraced themselves for all time by their genocide of the Armenian population, and suffered the indignity of Allied occupation of their capital, Istanbul.

Sultan Mehmed V proclaimed a jihad against the British that most Muslims ignored, just as calls for jihad since 2011 against the Alawite usurper, Bashar al-Assad, failed to rouse the Sunni masses of Syria's main population centers, Damascus and Aleppo. Assad made his own error from the day when he allowed his security services to fire on unarmed demonstrators in the belief that, as in the past, fear would send them home. They did not go home. They went to war.

Elia Samman, a member of the recently legalized wing of the Syrian Socialist Nationalist Party (SSNP) that seeks to unite all the states of Greater Syria, participated in the early demonstrations against the regime in 2011. Within a month of the first rallies in the southern desert town of Dera'a, he detected a significant change: "On 18 April, at the demonstrations in Homs, the biggest banner said, 'No to Iran. No to Hezbollah. We need a Muslim leader who feels God.' "

"A Muslim leader who feels God" was code for a Sunni Muslim to replace Assad as leader of Syria, in which 70 percent of the population are Sunni. At the

time, Iran and Hezbollah did not concern most dissidents, who regarded Assad's alliances with the two Shiite
powers as less important than their demands for genuine
elections, multiparty democracy, a free press, an independent judiciary, and the end of elite corruption that
was crippling the economy. Samman recalled:

> A couple of months later, we observed weapons [being
> distributed] under the guise of "protecting the demon-
> strators." When the violence became predominant, we
> told our members not to participate.

Within the year, the government's use of force and the
rise of armed groups in the opposition made public
protest both impossible and irrelevant. Jihadists took
over the rhetoric of the opposition, and democrats
had no place on either side of the barricades. The
population of Syria hemorrhaged to the four corners
of the world.

Europe's leaders, who had resisted wave after wave
of Syrian refugees until a drowned Syrian Kurdish
child's photograph embarrassed them into action in
early September, are again speaking of a diplomatic

solution that requires the agreement of the US, Russia, Iran, Saudi Arabia, Qatar, and Turkey. There has been much shuttling by Syrian oppositionists, Syrian intelligence chiefs, Russian and American diplomats, and Saudi princes. What is happening recalls the so-called peace process that has failed to break the Israeli–Palestinian impasse for the past twenty years. A senior Syrian official, who asked me not to publish his name, said, "We are at the threshold of a joint American–Russian effort with the UN to get the Syrian government and opposition into a collective effort against terrorism."

This is optimistic fantasy, given that the US will not coordinate any of its policies with the Assad regime in order to defeat ISIS. Moreover, neither the US nor Russia has budged from its initial position about Bashar al-Assad. The Russians insist he must stay, and the Americans demand that he go. Although they speak about negotiations, which ISIS gains in Syria and Iraq have made more urgent, they are not negotiating. Instead, they support the combatants' efforts to kill one another and turn more Syrians into refugees. A prominent Syrian oppositionist in exile told me that he explained to Russian Foreign Minister Sergei Lavrov that, for the opposition to fight against "terrorism" along with the Syrian army, "you would have to restructure the army." When I said that Assad would refuse to restructure the army, the oppositionist conceded, "Okay. That's why the war would never end."

Turkey, which probably has the most local influence in Syria, is using its professed war against ISIS as a smokescreen to attack Kurds, the most effective fighters to date against ISIS in Syria, Iraq, or Turkey itself. Egypt's President Abdel Fattah el-Sisi has suddenly thrown his hand in with Assad against the same sort of fundamentalists he overthrew and is imprisoning at home. He and Assad now share what Assad called "a joint vision" on security issues. The Syria war is a free-for-all in which everyone pursues his own interests to the detriment of the Syrians themselves.

At the end of *Seferberlik* in 1918, Britain and France occupied Syria and partitioned it into the statelets that have failed their populations ever since. No one knows where this war is leading or what today's children will pass on to the next generation. During the conflict of a century ago, the exiled poet Khalil Gibran watched from Boston, and wrote in "Dead Are My People":

My people and your people, my Syrian

Brother, are dead . . . What can be

Done for those who are dying?

Our Lamentations will not satisfy their

Hunger, and our tears will not quench

Their thirst; what can we do to save

Them from between the iron paws of

Hunger?

The United Nations' latest *Report of the Independent International Commission of Inquiry on the Syrian Arab Republic* paints a depressing portrait of the population's unimaginable torment at the hands of government and opposition forces alike. The regime drops barrel bombs in Aleppo, and the rebels respond with gas canisters of explosives and shrapnel. ISIS rapes and brutalizes Yazidi women whom it has declared slaves to be bought and sold. The regime's security services practice torture on an industrial scale. Both sides besiege villages, and both sides commit massacres. The UN report's horrific war crimes should be sufficient for the outside powers to budge and call a halt to this war. What are they waiting for?

EPILOGUE

ON 17 DECEMBER 1983, A FRENCH NEWS cameraman burst into the bar of Beirut's Commodore Hotel, where his colleagues gathered most evenings. "At last," he shouted, cupping both hands upwards, "someone with balls!" French warplanes had just bombed the town of Baalbek, site of magnificent Roman ruins but also of a Shiite Muslim militant barracks. This was France's revenge for the killing of 58 French troops by a suicide bomber four weeks earlier. On the same morning the French died, the United States had lost 241 American service personnel, most of them US Marines, to another suicide bomber. So far, Washington had not responded. We learned later that Defense Secretary Caspar Weinberger, who was against sending Marines to Lebanon in the first place, had dissuaded President Ronald Reagan from bombing Lebanon until there was evidence to prove who had done it.

France's bombardment satisfied one French cameraman. It changed nothing, except for the civilians and militants who died in Baalbek. When the US finally bombed eastern Lebanon in December, Syrian air defenses downed a Navy A-6 Intruder. The pilot, Lieutenant Mark Lange, died when his parachute malfunctioned. The navigator-bombardier, Lieutenant Robert O. Goodman, became a prisoner for 31 days until the Syrians released him to Reverend Jesse Jackson. And that was that.

In February 1984, the French and American forces of the ill-advised Multinational Force left Lebanon. French President François Mitterrand's promise to remain in defiance of those who had murdered his soldiers was forgotten, as was President Reagan's commitment to peace in Lebanon. The civil war, already in its eighth year, did not end until 1990. The parties behind the bombing of the French and American troops, the Hezbollah militia and its backers, Iran and Syria, emerged more or less victorious. In fact, Syria had proven itself so powerful in Lebanon that the US approved its military occupation to keep order. Syria went too far by assassinating former Lebanese Prime Minister Rafic Hariri in February 2005, and its troops were forced to evacuate the country two months later.

In 2015, in the aftermath of the November attacks in Paris, supporters of American, French and British bombing in Syria exulted that these western powers were showing their muscles, but there is every probability that they will balls it up. They have so far made a mess of Syria since they involved themselves in the vain attempt to bring down President Bashar al-Assad in 2011. Instead Islamic State fanatics emerged as the dominant power within the anti-Assad forces. They are not anti-dictatorship so much as anti-minority, particularly the ruling quasi-Shiite Alawite minority. The Western powers tolerated IS crimes, until IS turned from its bases in Syria and seized about a third of the American protectorate of Iraq. It was then that the US, to save the Kurdish capital at Erbil and the national capital of Baghdad, first bombed IS positions. Since then, other countries, including the Russians, who sought to save their Syrian protectorate, have joined the crusade against IS.

IS has turned around and murdered people from most of the countries that have challenged it: Shiite civilians in Iraq and Syria; Kurdish and leftwing Turkish peace demonstrators in Ankara; passengers on a Russian airliner over Egypt; Shiites, because of Hezbollah's involvement, in Beirut; and more than 120 innocents in Paris.

These international attacks, as well as the oppression and terror that IS has inflicted on large parts of Syria and Iraq, do not call for a response. They do not call for revenge. They do not call for gestures of the kind that British Prime Minister David Cameron succeeded in ramming through the UK Parliament in Westminster in early December. They do not call for Europe and the US to deny shelter to refugees who are fleeing from IS terror that the world ignored when it was confined to Syria. They do not call for further erosion of privacy and other rights closer to home.

The Islamic State's international attacks call for a strategy. If the goal is to eliminate IS from the territory it rules in Iraq and Syria, and from which it plots murder elsewhere, the forces opposed to it must come together. It took more than 100 dead in Paris and 224 passengers on a Russian airliner for France and Russia to coordinate their air strikes in Syria. What will it take for the US to do the same?

Air strikes, however, do not win wars. Warplanes drop bombs, meaning they function as airborne artillery. No military doctrine holds that artillery alone can conquer territory. That takes forces on the ground. The ground forces exist in both Syria and Iraq, and they are not from the western world. The Syrian Army, though odious to many Syrians and to the western powers, is the strongest of these and has weathered four and a half years of war without breaking up. It lost territory to IS in northeast Syria and at Palmyra, and it has reclaimed some of it with Russian air support. The Kurds of Iraq, supported by Kurds from Turkey and Syria and by US air strikes, have clawed back most of the territory that IS seized from them last year. The Shiite militias in southern Iraq, which filled the vacuum left by mass desertions from the US-created Iraqi Army, with Iranian support and American air cover saved Baghdad from IS conquest and regained lost ground. The war requires infantry, but not American, British and French troops. Nothing would turn Iraqis and Syrians to the jihadists more quickly than a western invasion.

Those of us who witnessed the Iraqi uprising of 1991, when Kurds and Shiites used the demoralization of Saddam Hussein's army in Kuwait to liberate 14 of Iraq's 18 provinces, know that it had more potential to save the country than the American-led invasion of 2003 did. The US pulled the plug on that rebellion in March 1991, and it launched its own bid to control Iraq in 2003, one that it is still paying for.

One step would not involve any combat at all: sever the supply route between IS and the outside world through Turkey. Turkey is an ally, but no friend. Its open border with Syria is the jihadis' lifeline. Without it, the weapons and ammunition the jihadis seized from the Iraqi Army last year would not have been enough for them to defend all their territory. Without it, jihadis trained in Syria would not have passed easily into Europe to murder civilians. Without it, the local forces whose shared hatred of the jihadis—who include the Syrian Army, the Kurds and all of Syria's and Iraq's other minorities, Iraq's majority Shiite population, secular Sunnis in Syria and Iraq and Lebanon's Hezbollah—would have stood a better chance of defeating them.

Diplomacy is better than war, and the outside powers that have been using Syria to fight their proxy wars must agree in Geneva or Vienna that enough is enough. The US, Russia, Iran, Turkey, Britain, France, Saudi Arabia and Qatar have all played their parts in destroying Syria. It is up to them to end this war that has cost as many as 310,000 lives. No one is winning. No one can win. They provide their clients with the means to fight the war. And they can cut them off.

Since March 2011, when the first protests began in Syria, the question has been what is to be done with President Bashar al-Assad. The reason the West, Saudi Arabia and Israel wanted to dispose of him had nothing to do with dictatorship or repression. Nearly all Arab governments are repressive dictatorships, but only Syria was not a US satellite. Only Syria had a strategic alliance with Iran, dating to Hafez al-Assad's decision to support Iran against Saddam Hussein in 1980, long before the West declared him a pariah. Syria supported Hezbollah in Lebanon, where it repelled Israel's invasion in 2006. And the US still had a score to settle with Hezbollah, which turned out to have staged the bombing of the marines in October 1983, as well as of the US Embassy the previous April, and to have kidnapped American citizens like myself in the years that followed.

Thus Assad had to go. The price was a conflagration that pits the world's two superpowers against each other in Syria's skies, and at the same time provides the landscape for Iran and Saudi Arabia to force their competing fantasies of "true" Islam on recalcitrant Syrians. This in turn has sent innocent refugees and guilty suicide bombers to every corner of the world. The wars in Iraq and Syria are destroying both countries, and the outside powers are escalating their armed involvement rather than finding a diplomatic settlement that grows more elusive with each day's delay. "During the Cold War, almost 20 million people died in Third World conflicts fueled largely by U.S.-Soviet competition," wrote Cato Institute visiting research fellow Brad Stapleton in October 2015. "That dismal history of proxy warfare suggests that more arms is not the answer in Syria." Yet more arms are what the US, Russia, Turkey, Saudi Arabia, Qatar and Iran are providing.

In July of 2015, four months before IS bombs and bullets massacred innocent civilians in Beirut and Paris, I wrote on *The Intercept* website,

> A friend of mine in Aleppo, who refuses to leave despite
> the battles in his once beautiful city, told me over the

telephone, "You have sent hell to us." That is, he blames me as a Westerner for putting the jihadis in his midst. The day cannot be far off when the jihadi militants, like the poor refugees whom they and the regime have displaced, will bring that hell back to us.

And so the jihadis did on a Russian airliner over the Sinai, in a Shiite suburb of Beirut and on the streets of Paris.

And so the jihadis will again, until peace is restored to Iraq and Syria. Peace, not war, will be the downfall of the Islamic State.

AFTERWORD

COULD SYRIA'S REVOLUTION HAVE BEEN different? At its birth in the spring of 2011, it promised a better, freer life for Syria's people. Syrian aspirations resonated with lovers of liberty everywhere: an end to government corruption and arbitrary arrest; an independent judiciary; a free press; equality before the law; abolition of torture; genuine elections leading to legitimate authority; and democratic institutions responsible to the governed. The state responded with arrests and violence. Dissidence evolved into war.

In lands remote from Syria, humanitarian interventionists, neoconservative ideologues and obtuse liberals raised their voices in support of the Syrian revolution. None of them had previously demonstrated sympathy for Syria or its people. They had withheld their support for Syria's legal claims to the Golan Heights, which Israel has occupied since 1967, and thus for the return of its 150,000 displaced residents and their descendants. In 2011, the State Department, Whitehall and the Quai d'Orsay discovered the legitimate rights of the Syrian people and made them a priority. Word went out to their intelligence agencies and regional client states that the rebels, from wherever they came, would have arms, money and training. And so it came to pass.

Among the external opinion formers and policymakers were cynical opportunists. Their objective, as Zbigniew Brzezinski's was with the Soviets in Afghanistan, to bleed Syria. It was also to break its strategic alliances with Russia and Iran. The rebels' cheering section included self-proclaimed idealists, "useful idiots" who did not foresee that their new Syria must contain a good deal of the old Syria with the added trappings of Wahhabi revanchism. They preferred not to acknowledge, much as a previous generation of fellow travelers closed its eyes to mass executions and show trials in Stalin's Soviet Union, that those who would fight hardest against the Syrian regime would inevitably be those unafraid of death. Such fundamentalists had always opposed Syria's regimes because of their secular rather than their dictatorial nature.

Those who eventually captured the revolution dropped its original objectives in favor of supplanting a secular dictatorship with a dictatorial theocracy. The revolution was defeated from within, albeit with much assistance from outside powers motivated by anything but the good of the Syrian people.

Thirty-five years earlier, a coalition of progressive movements in neighboring Lebanon issued similar demands for reform. It may be helpful to recall what happened in Lebanon during a 15-year civil war that, despite an estimated 150,000 deaths and the transfer of populations into sectarian ghettos, left the corrupt antebellum system intact. In 1975, the year that Lebanon's war erupted, there seemed nothing incongruous about a revolution led by what the French press called *Islamo-progressites*. The world had yet to witness the Islamic revolutions in Iran, Sudan, Libya, Egypt and Yemen. Those movements were more reactionary than progressive, less liberating than despotic. Yet, in those naïve times, progress and Islam did not seem self-contradictory. Indeed, Lebanon's Christian parties, despite having sponsored social security and pension reform in parliament, resisted change, while Muslim militias waved the banner of revolutionary progress. It was a time when a Marxist historian, Maxime Rodin, could write about Islam both critically and sympathetically without fear of assassination.

Revolutions that begin with the goal of liberating people from the dead weight of an oppressive past often lead to a more oppressive present. Ideals give way to expediency. Those most likely to seize control of popular forces are pitiless rather than compassionate, well financed rather than independent, more conspiratorial than collaborative. Those who trust their fellow revolutionaries suffer for it, while the victors are those who first destroy the enemies on their own side. So it was in Lebanon; so it would be in Syria.

The Palestinian commando groups that had been expelled from Jordan in 1970 took their revolution to Lebanon, where it flourished. Initially secular, democratic and socialist, the Palestinian national movement threatened the sectarian, dictatorial and pseudo-capitalist oligarchies of the Arab world more than it ever did its ostensible enemy, Israel. The rich Arab oil states, notably Saudi Arabia and Kuwait, funded nationalist Palestinians like Yasser Arafat of Al Fateh as a counterweight to the more dynamic socialist movements led by George Habash and Nayef Hawatmeh. The leaders of the Popular and Democratic Fronts for the Liberation of Palestine happened to be Christians and secularists, whose followers included more Muslims than Christians. The princes, sheikhs and mullahs of the Arabian Peninsula rejected them and their philosophy. Saudi financing enabled Arafat's Fateh, with its incoherent ideology and tensions between its secular and Islamist adherents, to claim the leadership of all Palestinians. Al Fateh used Saudi money to dominate its rivals in the Palestinian movement and to lead the Lebanese Left to self-destruction.

The idealists who demanded structural change in Lebanon's body politic lost ground to the partisans of sectarian identity. From seeking an end to the distribution of political spoils from the presidency down to postal clerks by sect, they demanded merely a larger share of the spoils for Muslims, specifically Sunni Muslims from outside the traditional elite that had shared power with the Maronite Christians since the state's independence. Instead of making all Lebanese equal before the law, as the socialists had proposed, they would recalibrate the distribution of state offices to reflect changed demographics. What had been a principle surrendered to the familiar horse-trading that Lebanon had inherited from the Ottoman Empire and the French Mandate. It was barely reform, certainly not worth killing or dying for.

In the mid-1970s, the Left in Lebanon, as in Chile and other countries where popular movements challenged oligarchies dependent on the United States, met overwhelming external resistance. The US approved Saudi Arabia's policy of co-opting and taming the Palestinian revolution and, with it, Lebanon's National Movement. Saudi Arabia would go on to fund Islamic opposition to social change as far afield as Nicaragua, Afghanistan and, most recently, Syria.

As well as bolstering nationalist opposition to socialism, Saudi Arabia used the Islamists to undercut nationalism. Islamic revanchist movements funded by Saudi Arabia's oil wealth resisted economic and social reform in Gamal Abdel Nasser's Egypt in the 1950s and opposed education for women in Syria 20 years later. In

Lebanon, they failed to represent the most impoverished segment of society, the Shiite Muslim peasantry
whom Israel in its military onslaught against the
Palestinians was exiling to the shanty towns of Beirut's
southern outskirts.

Arab nationalism, with its commitment to equality
among Muslims, Christians and Jews, died in the Arab
versus Arab bloodletting on the streets of Beirut in the
1970s. One motivating idea remained: Islam in political forms dictated by Saudi Arabia for the Sunnis and
by Iran, after its 1979 revolution, for the Shiites. A
political division within Islam that had lain dormant
for centuries would torment Lebanon, Iraq, Yemen,
Bahrain, Syria and the eastern province of Saudi
Arabia.

In the spring of 1976, the western half of Beirut
was infected with the revolutionary ethos that saw the
rich, like Italians fearful of the *Brigate Rosse* in the
same era, hiding their jewelry and luxury cars from
the envious glare of a roused proletariat. There were
echoes of Orwell's Catalonia in both the idealism of
young zealots and the cynicism of power-hungry
aspiring dictators. The US Secretary of State, Henry

Kissinger, recognized the threat to American dominance, as he did in so many other countries, and fashioned a solution in the form of a Syrian invasion to protect the embattled old guard and control the excesses of the Palestinian-Lebanese rebels. The revolution died, but the war raged for another 14 years. The war ended, but only after two Israeli invasions and countless massacres. Foreign powers imposed a settlement at a conference in Taif, Saudi Arabia, in October 1989. By then, most Lebanese were willing to accept any outcome that allowed them to drive to work without fear of snipers, car bombs, artillery or kidnapping.

Lebanon, like Syria, saw democratic, secular dreams vanish into a sectarian maelstrom that ravaged the country and left it vulnerable to foreign invasion and local brutality. Yes, Lebanon's old system encouraged corruption. Yes, there was injustice. Yes, a majority suffered from inequalities. Yet changing the system was no excuse to shred the fabric of a society that, for all its flaws, was tolerant of different creeds and political beliefs. Two revolutions perished in Lebanon, the Palestinian and the Lebanese. Security became more important than freedom, if only because so much freedom permitted the anarchic rule of kidnappers, gangsters, drug dealers, gun runners and fanatics. In the absence of central authority, the only states on Lebanon's borders, Syria and Israel, occupied different halves of the country. The only militia to survive the war as an armed force was Hezbollah, a sectarian grouping of religious Shiite Muslims that represents Iran and the perpetuation of sectarian politics in Lebanon.

One way to view the fanatic Islamicization of the Syrian revolution after 2011 is that it was the inevitable form of a rebellion inspired and financed by Saudi Wahhabism that sought not democracy but the elimination of rule by Alawite "infidels." Another is that fratricidal violence marginalizes moderation, renders compromise impossible and pushes forward the most brutal actors. What was more surprising than the rise of fanatics within the revolution was that such disparate opposition forces had found any common ground at all. Like the leftists opposed to the Shah of Iran in 1979, Syria's democrats saw their Islamist allies dispose of them and their beliefs when they were no longer needed. If the regime fell, the victors would replace it with a theocratic dictatorship that would purge the country of its diversity, its minorities, its dissidents and its tolerance.

The Syrian revolution lacked strategic vision because it began without any objective beyond reforming or replacing a regime that had nurtured as many allies as enemies. Too many rebel leaders sold themselves, as most Palestinian leaders did, to external paymasters for any one of them to establish popular, unifying credentials. Hundreds of armed groups came into being, sponsored by the United States, Britain, France, Saudi Arabia, Qatar and Turkey. The regime, which had almost 50 years to perfect mechanisms of control, played its cards better than rebels with no experience of government, no roots in social work and little experience of combat. Fighters with battle scars from Chechnya, Bosnia, Iraq, Afghanistan, Pakistan, Algeria and Libya dominated the rebel side of battlefield. When they trod across the border into Iraq and threatened American interests, the Obama administration responded with air strikes. Yet it did not admit it was wrong about Syria, the strength of the regime or the relative strength of fanaticism within the opposition. That would have meant admitting it was wrong to assume the regime was so unpopular and weak it would fall with a small push before the opposition turned from early reformist demands to radical Islamism.

Robert Ford, the former US ambassador to Syria who had championed the revolution and encouraged its militarization, was a rare official who admitted that the policy he had espoused was mistaken. He told a conference in Washington in January 2015, after nearly 200,000 Syrian deaths and the displacement of a third of the population, "The people we have backed have not been strong enough to hold their ground against the Nusra Front." If the US could not achieve its goals in Syria, he added, "then we have to just walk away and say there's nothing we can do about Syria." This is rich coming from an ambassador whose policies helped to create the fanatic groups controlling large regions of Syria and Iraq. To America's policy-making adolescents, the world is a plaything to abandon when it breaks.

The rebels, using weapons made in America, paid for by Saudi Arabia and funneled through Turkey, imposed a vision of society that took no account of Syrian diversity and mutual respect among its peoples. Syria, as history records, welcomed the Armenian victims of Turkey's genocide after World War I and had long been home to heterodox forms of Islam.

The goal of the self-proclaimed Islamic State and Jebhat al-Nusra was to make Syria something it never was: an extension of Saudi Arabia. No one heeded Nietzsche's warning, quoted early in the revolution by Masalit Mati, writer of the satirical, anti-Assad *Top Goon* puppet show: "Be careful when you fight the monsters, lest you become one."

The United States, with its European and Arab allies, had its own purposes in Syria. It strains belief that the US, Saudi Arabia and Qatar opposed Bashar al-Assad because he was a dictator or because his cousins were taking the lion's share of the country's wealth. The countries that crushed popular dissent against the royal family in Bahrain could not claim to believe in democracy for any Arab country. The US opposed Assad, as did the Saudis and Qataris, because he would not relinquish the alliance with Iran that gave him a strategic asset against Israel. Israel had occupied part of Syria since

1967 and showed no sign of relinquishing its hold or permitting the exiled inhabitants and their descendants to return. The Arab monarchies, which had sought to dominate Syria since it achieved independence from France in 1946, saw in Iran an adversary for control of Syria and, through Hezbollah, Lebanon. To remove Assad was to eliminate Iranian influence in the Arab world.

In the midst of the Syrian war and despite Israel's desire to humiliate Iran, the US opened a door to the regime in Tehran. Negotiations to regulate the Iranian nuclear program improved relations between the long-time adversaries. As American business scented an opportunity to return to the lucrative Iranian market, the raison d'être for America to eliminate Iran's only Arab ally evaporated. US policy in Syria has floundered ever since.

Hopes for a negotiated end to the war receded with the deterioration in America's relationship with Vladimir Putin's Russia, Assad's only ally apart from Iran and the regime in Baghdad, over Ukraine and the eastern expansion of the North Atlantic Treaty Organization (NATO). The US, Russia, the Syrian regime and much of the Syrian opposition came to

Geneva in January 2014 with no plan, no inclination to end Syrian agony and no purpose other than pushing their own goals to the detriment of a population that was enduring the daily reality of death, maiming, exodus and oppression from both camps.

Renewed talks in Vienna at the end of October 2015 produced platitudes from the outside powers and set a target of January 1, 2016, for negotiations to begin between the Assad regime and the opposition. As the target came within view, its sponsors pushed it back to January 25 and continued to pour arms and explosives into Syria with the ostensible goal of negotiating from positions of strength.

Meanwhile, the dominant force in the Syrian revolution proclaimed itself a caliphate, beheaded innocent prisoners, raped and enslaved women, hurled young men from towers because of their sexual preferences and burned alive a young Jordanian soldier who fought for his country. This is where superpower, Turkish and Arab policies have led. Where will they take Syria next?

ACKNOWLEDGEMENTS

MY DEBT TO THOSE WHO OVER MANY years have taught me about Syria is greater than I can ever repay. I am particularly grateful for the education I received from the late Patrick Seale, John Cooley and Peter Jennings, all of whom wrote presciently about Syria throughout their illustrious careers. I must also thank the Agence France Presse correspondent in Beirut, Rana Moussaoui, for her insights into a conflict she has been reporting from Syria since its birth in March 2011; Jim Muir of the BBC; David Hirst, formerly of the *Guardian*; and Jonathan Steele of the *Guardian*.

Most of those I need to thank are Syrian friends who have endured with patience the slow destruction of their country while giving of their time to explain it to this outsider: Armen Mazloumian of the famed Baron's

Hotel in Aleppo, Magdy Jubaili, George Saliba, Tony Touma, Georges Antaki, Ghaith Armanazi, Mounzer Nazha, Sara Shamma, Colette Khoury, the human rights lawyer Anwar Bounni, Samir Khaterji, Bishop Armash Nabaldian, Monsignor Boutros Marayati, Jihad Makdissi, Lina Sinjab and Jack Barsoum of the BBC, Roulla Rouqbi, Nabil Sukkar, Nashwa Mraish, Orwa Nyarabia, Zaidoun Zoabi, Khaled Khaleefa, Nora Arissian, Missak Baghboudarian, Maia Mamarbashi, Yazan Abdallah, Bouthaina Shaaban, Reem Haddad and Emma Abbas. I hope that it will soon be possible to repay the kindness of the Greek and Syriac Orthodox arch-bishops of Aleppo, Boulos Yazigi and Gregorios Yohanna Ibrahim, who were kidnapped in Syria in April 2013. They did all they could to prevent the spread of hatred and fanaticism in their country and became two of among millions of victims in a war that should never have begun. There are other Syrians that I can thank by name only at the risk of their lives, so I must acknowledge them here without revealing their identities. They know how much I owe them. My thanks must also go to countless United Nations staff and aid workers, who have been unfailing in their courtesy in difficult circumstances. I think particularly of Moktar Lamani, Yacub El Hilo, Emilio Tamburi Quinteiro, Matthew Hollingworth, Tamara Zayyat, Hussam El Saleh and Karin McLennan, although this list is anything but exhaustive. I would also like to thank Walid Bey Jumblatt for his many insights into Syrian history and his caustic observations on its political life, as well as his wife Nora, a loyal Syrian of whom her country can be proud.

Without the support of Robert Silvers at the *New York Review of Books*, I would not have been able to spend as much time as I was able to in Syria after 2011. He is as gracious and conscientious an editor as any writer could hope to please. I must also express my gratitutde to Jamie Stern-Weiner for his meticulous editing of my often unwieldy text and to Colin Robinson for suggesting this book and bringing it to fruition at OR Books. I would like also to thank Leo Hollis and Mark Martin at Verso for their valiant work in bringing out the new and updated edition. My thanks must also go to my literary agent, Ed Victor, who represents me and countless others with the aplomb and style for which he is justifiably famous. I owe Patrick Cockburn a drink for his unjustifiably laudatory foreword.

CHARLES GLASS is an author, journalist and broadcaster, who specializes in the Middle East. He made headlines when taken hostage for 62 days in Lebanon by Shi'a militants in 1987, while writing a book during his time as ABC's News chief Middle East correspondent. He writes regularly for the *New York Review of Books*, *Harper's*, the *London Review of Books* and the *Spectator*. He is the author of *Tribes with Flags*, *Money for Old Rope*, *The Tribes Triumphant*, *The Northern Front*, *Americans in Paris*, and *Deserters: A Hidden History of World War II*.